What Do You Think?

Introductory exercises
in inferential comprehension

Eric Williams

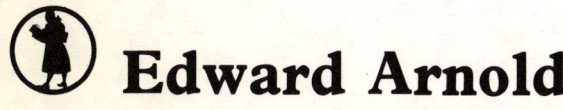 Edward Arnold

© Eric Williams 1982

First published 1982
by Edward Arnold (Publishers) Ltd
41 Bedford Square
London WC1B 3DQ

British Library Cataloguing in Publication Data

Williams, Eric
    What do you think? introductory exercises in
    inferential comprehension.
    1. English language—Composition and exercises
    428.2   PE1112

ISBN 0-7131-0695-6

Acknowledgements
The Publishers wish to thank the following for permission to use copyright material:
The Bodley Head for Rosemary Sutcliff: *Beowulf: Dragon Slayer* and Betsy Byars: *The Eighteenth Emergency*; Chatto and Windus Ltd for Susan Cooper: *Dawn of Fear*; Daily Express, Daily Mail, Daily Mirror, Daily Telegraph and The Times for their articles; Penelope Lively: *The Ghost of Thomas Kempe*; Methuen Children's Books for Anne Holm: *I am David* and Ivan Southall: *Let the Balloon Go* and Penguin Books Ltd for Clive King: *The Night the Water Came*.

Introductory exercises in inferential comprehension by Eric Williams:
Secrets
What Do You Think?
Reading Beyond the Lines

Filmset in 11/12 Compugraphic Plantin by RDL, 26 Mulgrave Road, Sutton, Surrey.
Printed in Great Britain by Spottiswoode Ballantyne Limited, Colchester and London.

Preface

'Everyone would agree that additional attention should be given to children whose progress is unsatisfactory, but we would strongly emphasize the need to stimulate average and above average children to greater achievement. This means that the teacher should spend time with them individually, for it is not only the poor readers who warrant attention of this kind. A good deal of incentive can be provided by well organized small group work, where the interaction draws upon shared experiences in reading. The children can be encouraged to discuss what they are reading, to ask questions and offer answers, and to compare their ideas of what the book said. They should become accustomed quite early to going back to the printed word and looking more carefully at something on which their talk has focussed.' (Bullock Report, 7.31)

This book is intended to provide the teacher with starting-points for group discussion that will encourage pupils to read more closely and critically. It is aimed principally, but not exclusively, at the 11–13 age range and can be used either independently or in conjunction with *Reading Beyond the Lines* where approaches introduced here are developed further. The exercises in both books are concerned primarily with inferential comprehension, which demands thinking and imagination which go beyond what is printed. Throughout, pupils are asked to use clues in the text to help them deduce aspects of meaning, and three fundamental questions are implied:

What do you think?

Why do you think so?

Will you read out the part which proves it?

Discussion of the passages can be led by the teacher working with a class, the pupils having written the answers beforehand. In practice, however, these exercises have proved to be particularly effective when it has been possible to discuss the answers to the questions in small groups, to promote reflective reading as urged by Lunzer and Gardner in The *Effective Use of Reading*.

The exercises have been arranged in eight units. These, broadly speaking, appear in order of increasing difficulty, but there is no need for the teacher to feel that the book needs to be worked through as a course. The passages collected here can be used independently in conjunction with other resource materials. As in *Reading Beyond the Lines*, there is a preponderance of substantial extracts from fiction that is readily available to pupils in paperback form; these have been arranged in a sequence that will encourage comparison, so that each individual passage can be read in relation to those surrounding it. It is hoped that pupils will want to read the complete novels from which extracts are taken; missing words and titles are listed as an appendix as is a list of further suggestions for reading.

E.W.

1

Here is the opening of a story called *I Am David*. Read it carefully, thinking about what we find out about David here. Answer the questions as you come to them.

David lay quite still in the darkness, listening to the men's low muttering. But this evening he was aware of their voices only as a vague meaningless noise in the distance, and he paid no attention to what they were saying.

'You must get away tonight,' the man had told him. 'Stay awake so that you're ready just before the guard's changed. When you see me strike a match, the current will be cut off and you can climb over – you'll have half a minute for it, no more.'

In his mind's eye David saw once again the grey bare room he knew so well. He saw the man and was conscious, somewhere in the pit of his stomach, of the hard knot of hate he felt whenever he saw him. The man's eyes were small, repulsive, light in colour, their expression never changing; his face was gross and fat. David had known him all his life, but he never spoke to him more than was barely necessary to answer his questions; and though he had known his name for as long as he could remember, he never said anything but 'the man' when he spoke about him or thought of him. Giving him a name would be like admitting that he knew him; it would place him on an equal footing with the others.

1 What have you found out about David from reading these opening paragraphs?
2 As you read on, make a note of any further information you can find about:
(a) David;
(b) where he is; and
(c) how he feels about the man.

But that evening he had spoken to him. He had said, 'And if I don't escape?'

The man had shrugged his shoulders. 'That'll be none of my business. I have to leave here tomorrow, and whatever my successor may decide to do about you, I shan't be able to interfere. But you'll soon be a big lad, and there's need in a good many places for those strong enough to work.'

David knew only too well that those other places would not be any better than the camp where he now was. 'And if I get away without being caught, what then?' he had asked.

'Just by the big tree in the thicket that lies on the road out to the mines, you'll find a bottle of water and a compass. Follow the compass southwards till you get to Salonica, and then when no one's looking go on board a ship and hide. You'll have to stay hidden while the ship's at sea, and you'll need the water. Find a ship that's bound for Italy, and when you get there go north till you come to a country called Denmark – you'll be safe there.'

David had very nearly shown his astonishment, but he controlled himself, and hiding his feelings merely said, 'I don't know what a compass is.'

The man had shown him one, telling him that the four letters indicated north, south, east and west, and that the needle, which swung freely, always pointed in the same direction. Then he had added. 'The half minute the current's cut off is intended for you. If you try to take anyone with you, you can be sure that neither of you will get away. And now clear off before you're missed.'

David did not know what possessed him to say it – he had never asked the man for anything, partly because he knew it would be of no use, but chiefly because he would not – when you hated someone, you did not ask him for anything. But tonight he had done it: when he reached the door, he turned round, and looking straight into that coarse heavy face said, 'I'd like a piece of soap.'

For a moment there had been complete silence in that bare grey room. Then the man picked up a cake of soap that lay by the side of the wash-basin in the corner and threw it on the table. All he said was, 'Now go.'

So David had gone, as quickly as it was possible to go without appearing to be in a hurry.

The men's muttering was fainter now – some of them must have fallen asleep. The camp's latest arrival was still talking. David recognized his voice because it was less flat and grating than the others. Whenever the newcomer dozed off to sleep, he was seized with a nightmare, and then they would all wake up again. The night before, this had happened just before the guard was changed, but if he took longer to fall asleep this evening, then it might be possible for David to slip out before the others were wakened again.

David was not yet sure whether he would make the attempt. He tried to work out why the man had told him to do it. It was certainly a trap: just as he was climbing over, the searchlight would suddenly swing round and catch him in its beam, and then they would shoot. Perhaps something pleasant was going to happen tomorrow and the man wanted him shot first. David had always known that the man hated him, just as much as David hated *him* in return. On the other hand, nothing pleasant had ever yet happened in the camp that David could remember, and he was now twelve years old – it said so on his identity-card.

And then quite suddenly David decided he would do it. He had turned it over in his mind

until his head was in a whirl and he still could not understand why the man had told him to escape. Suppose it were a trap and they shot him, it would all be over quickly anyway. If you were fired at while trying to escape, you would be dead within a minute. Yes, David decided to try.

3(a) Discuss your answers to 1 and 2 with the person sitting next to you.
(b) How does David feel about the escape?
4(a) As you read on, notice how David's feelings change.
(b) What surprises him?

There could not be many minutes left now. Over in the guard-room he could hear them moving about and getting dressed, and he could hear the guard yawning as his pace grew slower. Then came the sound of new steps and David pressed himself even more closely against the wall. It was the man; the faint sleepy yellow light from the guard-room shone for a moment on his face as he passed the window. He went up to the guard, and David suddenly felt quite empty inside and was sure that he would be unable to move when the time came. Then he saw before him the endless succession of days, months and years that would pass if he did not. The waiting would kill him in the end, but it might take years. And it would grow worse and worse, all the time: David clenched his teeth so hard that he felt the muscles of his throat grow taut. Then the man struck a match.

Nineteen, twenty . . . the half minute would be up when he had counted slowly to thirty . . . David set his foot in a gap higher up the barbed wire . . . When would the searchlight come? They could not be certain of hitting him in the dark . . . and if they did not hurry he would be over.

A moment later he had touched the ground on the other side, and as he ran he said angrily to himself, 'What a fool you are! There's plenty of ground to cover yet – all this great flat stretch without so much as the stump of a tree for shelter. They'll wait till you've nearly reached the thicket . . . they'll think it more amusing if you believe you've almost got to safety.'

Why didn't they hurry up? The thought pounded through his head as every moment he expected to see the ground lit up in front of him. Then he stopped. He would run no more. When the beam of light caught him, they should see him walking away quite calmly. Then they would not enjoy it so much, they would feel cheated. The thought filled David with triumph.

When he was little, it had been his most burning desire to get the better of them, especially of the man. And now he would! They would be forced to shoot him as they watched him walking quietly away and taking no notice of them!

David was so taken up with his victory over them that he had gone a dozen yards past the spot where the thicket hid him from the camp before he realized that no one had fired. He stopped short. What could have happened? He turned, found a place where the thicket was thin enough to peer through and looked across at the low buildings outlined against the dark sky, like an even darker smudge of blackness. He could faintly hear the tread of the guard, but it came no nearer and sounded no different from usual, only farther off. Nothing at all appeared different.

David frowned in the darkness and stood for a moment undecided: it couldn't possibly . . .? He trotted on, following the edge of the thicket towards the big tree, running faster the nearer he got, and when he reached the tree he threw himself down on the ground, searching frantically with his hands round the trunk.

There was the bundle. David leaned up against the tree shivering with cold although it was not cold at all. The bundle was a piece of cloth wrapped round something and tied in a knot. He fumbled with the knot, but his fingers were clumsy and would not respond – and then he suddenly realized that he dared not undo it. There would be something dangerous inside the bundle . . . He tried to gather his thoughts together sufficiently to think what it might be, but his imagination did not get beyond a bomb.

It would make little difference, he thought desperately – a bullet or a bomb: it would soon be over, either way. Frantically, his fingers awkward, he struggled with the knot.

But there was no bomb in the cloth. It was a square handkerchief tied cross-wise over a bottle of water and a compass, just as the man had said. He barely managed to turn aside before he was sick.

Afterwards he felt carefully all round the square-shaped bundle. A bottle, a compass – there was something else. David's eyes had grown accustomed to the darkness: in the bundle there were also a box of matches, a large loaf of bread and a pocket-knife.

So the man had intended him to escape after all! A search-party would be sent out for him in the morning, but not before. The night was his, and it was up to him to make the most of it.

All this had taken only a few minutes, but to David it felt like hours. His hand closed tightly round the soap – he had not let go of it for a moment since he first got it. He recalled the hours he had spent that evening lying on his plank-bed listening to the muttered conversation of the men and thinking over what the man had said. He remembered, too, that it would be only a matter of time before he was caught again; but that, like everything else, no longer seemed important. All that mattered now was his bundle and the freedom of the night that lay ahead. Slowly he tucked the piece of soap into a corner of the handkerchief, laid the bottle, bread and knife on top, tied the ends together, took a firm grip on the knot and looked at the compass in his hand.

Then he ran.

---

5 Discuss your answers to (a) and (b) above with the person sitting next to you.

2

1 After you have read through the paragraph that follows, explain:
(a) what has happened in the past to bring about the scene described here;
(b) what you understand the words underlined to mean – you should be able to work out all of them by thinking about the rest of the paragraph.

Many hundreds of years before, a family of mighty warriors had gathered by <u>inheritance</u> and by strength in war an immense store of treasure, gold cups and crested helmets, arm-rings of earls and necklaces of queens, ancient swords and armour wrought with magic spells by the dwarf-kind long ago. A great war of many battles had carried away all this <u>kinsfolk</u> save one, and he, lonely and brooding on the fate of the precious things that he and his kin had gathered with such joy when he also should have gone by the <u>Dark Road</u>, made ready a secret <u>fastness</u> that he knew of, a cave under the headland that men called the Whale's ness. And there, little by little, he carried all his treasures and hid them within sounding of the sea, and made a death-song over them as over slain warriors, lamenting for the <u>thanes</u> who would drink from the golden cups and wield the mighty sword no more, for the hearths grown cold and the harps fallen silent and the halls abandoned to the foxes and the ravens.

2 The remainder of this passage has been divided into three sections. Read each section through twice. During the second reading make a list of the words that you think have been left out.

After you have made lists for all three sections, compare your choices with those made by other members of your class or group. How many different words can you find that would make sense? Which do you prefer?

A

When the man died the hoard was forgotten and lay _____ under the flank of the hill while the _____ centuries went by, until at last a fire-dragon, _____ a lair among the rocks, came upon the hidden entrance to the cave and _____ within, found the treasure. Because he had found it the fire-dragon thought that it was his, and he _____ it, heavy arm-ring and jewelled dagger and gold-wrought cup; and he _____ his slithering coils about it and lay _____ over it for three hundred years.

B

But at the end of that time a man who had angered his chieftain in some way and was fleeing from his _____ also found the hidden entrance among the rocks, and the golden _____ and the dragon sleeping.

Now through all those three hundred years the dragon had been _____ growing, until from snout to tail tip he was ten times as long as a man is _____ . Yet still he was not long enough completely to _____ the mound of treasure, and between snout and tail tip as he lay was a gap just wide enough to let through a man.

The fugitive saw the golden _____ of the hoard, and even while his brain _____ at the sight it seemed to him that here might be a way out of his desperate _____ . Creeping between snout and tail tip of the sleeping dragon, he caught up a golden cup, one great cup _____ like the sun with which to buy off his chieftain's wrath, and, _____ it to his breast, fled back the way he had come.

C

Presently the fire-dragon woke, and knew in the _____ of his waking that he had been robbed. Blindly, in grief and fury, he _____ about his beloved hoard, and knew by the smell that a man had been there. He crawled outside and _____ about the entrance to the cave and among the rocks, and found man's footprints; and when the dusk came down he _____ his great wings and flew out in search of the thief.

Night after night from that time forward he flew out, filled with _____ and seeking not only the thief but to _____ his vengeance on all men because it was a man who had robbed him. Far and wide he flew, from coast to coast of Geatland, _____ in his own fiery breath as though in mists of flame. Houses, men, trees and cattle, even the King's Hall itself, _____ up as his angry breath blew upon them, and at each sunrise when he returned to his lair, he left the _____ of his night's flying marked in black and _____ desolation across the land.

(You can compare your choice of words with those used by the author by consulting the lists on page 44. However, they have been arranged in alphabetical order, so you will still need to think about them!)

---

1 From reading these headlines, what do you think the news story is going to be about? What can you guess already about what happened?

FOUR MINUTE RAIDERS GRAB £$\frac{3}{4}$m

Shotgun fusillade at ambushed van

£750,000 TIN CAN RIP-OFF

Chain-saw gang in cash haul

Power-saw gang ambush van

Gang steals £750,000 after faking road crash

Bandits fire after ramming security van

TIN OPENER GANG GRAB £750,000

The same story appears on the following pages five times, as told in five different newspapers on the same day. Your task is to compare each version with the others, and think about which of the stories gives you the clearest description of what happened.

2 First of all read the first version on page 8 then find the answers to these questions. Write your answers in note form, as you will need them later on.

(a) How many men were in the gang? How was the job divided among them?
(b) How long did the robbery take?
(c) How much was stolen? Did the gang take all the money? If not, how much was left and why?
(d) Why would it have been difficult for any of the security men to have been able to identify the members of the gang later – for instance, when looking through photographs of criminals?
(e) How many men were in the security van?
(f) How many cars did the gang use in the raid? Which of these were stolen? What were the names of the makes of car they used?
(g) How did they stop the van? What did the men have to do to get the money from the van into a car?
(h) How did they make sure they were undisturbed by anyone else while they carried out their raid?
(i) How many people were injured? Did the gang have any weapons?
(j) How did the gang meet up before the raid and get away afterwards?
(k) Who raised the alarm? How far away was the nearest police station?
(l) How were the gang able to plan their raid so accurately?

A 10-MAN armed gang stole £750,000 in a four-minute raid on a security van in Sutton Lane, Banstead, Surrey, yesterday. They used a portable power saw to cut into the bodywork to get at the cash, but in their haste missed a further £100,000.

They used a stolen car to ram the van, owned by Security Express, punctured its wheels with shotgun fire, and smashed the radio linking it with the firm's headquarters.

One gang member, wearing a police-type uniform with a luminous jacket bearing the words "Police, slow," diverted traffic from the ambush scene, on an isolated stretch of Sutton Lane.

The gang, wearing goggles, crash helmets, balaclavas and scarves, staged their ambush from several cars.

As some fired at the vas's tyres and windows, others trundled a portable mechanical chainsaw, operated by a small petrol motor, from one of the cars.

This was used to cut open the side of the security vehicle. The The £750,000 was in 35 bags which they hurriedly loaded into their waiting vehicles.

"They missed four money bags which contained another £100,000," a spokesman for De La Rue, the Security Express parent company, said later.

7-vehicle convoy

None of the three-man security van crew was hurt in the firing.

Police learned later that the gang waited in seven vehicles in a car park at Lower Park Road, where people park when they are going for a walk through local woods.

The vehicles left in convoy some time after 1.15 p.m., which was about 20 minutes before the ambush.

The vehicles, in this order, were a dark blue Ford Escort van, a silver Ford Escort, a Granada, three Cortinas and a dark blue Sherpa van.

After the robbery the whole of the gang got into the Sherpa van and drove off through the grounds of Banstead Hospital to The Grange, opposite Greenacres School, where they transferred to two large cars, both believed to be Ford Granadas.

Road blocks

Staff and patients of Banstead Hospital saw two men abandon a car near one of the entrances and run off through the grounds. They made for another car, which drove away before staff had finished making a 999 call.

Road checks were set up by both Metropolitan and Surrey police.

The security van and the cars used in the ambush were taken to Banstead police station, which is about 300 yards from the scene, and examined by forensic experts.

Det. Chief Supt. James Sewell, head of Scotland Yard's recently formed Central Robbery Squad, in in charge of inquiries and has set up a temporary headquarters at Banstead police station.

Mrs Joyce Gammi, who lives about 50 yards from the ambush scene, said: "When I discovered what had happened I went into the lane and saw the security men standing by the van. Fortunately nobody was hurt but the man looked very shaken.

"I saw a policeman carrying a sawn-off shotgun, and a bag of money had been dropped on the footpath." She had heard "a few bumps and shots" but took little notice because workmen had been busy in the area.

Whenever possible, security van routes and timings are varied and details of the journey disclosed only at the latest possible moment to those concerned in the deliveries.

But the general nature of some of the deliveries and collections forces the van to take specific routes at specific times, such as regular delivery of wages or the collection of takings from shops and businesses daily.

This gives gangs the opportunity to observe, time and follow vans on regular runs to that the most favourable time and place for an ambush can be decided. Police believe such a plan was followed for yesterday's raid.

They are asking for information from anyone who may have noticed a strange car or van in the vicinity of the ambush point recently, particularly a week ago.

3 Now read a second version of the same story, and use your answers to the questions as a checklist for you to compare the two stories.

Make a list of

(a) any facts that are different from those you read in the first version (for instance, the number of cars used to ram the security van);

(b) any information that this version gives in addition to what you found out from reading A;

(c) any information in A that doesn't appear in B.

B

A gang with a split-second sense of timing yesterday stole £750,000 in four minutes. They staged a fake road accident, with a bogus policeman, to seal off a suburban road before ramming a Security Express van and holding its guards at gunpoint.

The gang cut through the van's armour plating with a chain saw to reach the money inside, then fled on foot to getaway cars near by. In their hurry they left £100,000 in the van.

The robbery is thought to be the biggest from a money consignment in road transit. At least eight men were involved.

The robbery happened in Sutton Lane, Banstead, Surrey, at lunchtime when two cars were hijacked near by and used to block the road. The owners were ordered to hand over their vehicles at gunpoint.

The gang then pretended that the stolen cars had crashed. "They even had a person lying in the road pretending to be injured", said Mr David Gannie, a witness.

As the security van entered the other end of the road a man wearing a luminous jacket and uniform bearing the words "Police slow" stepped into the street and prevented traffic from entering the area.

The security van crashed into the back of a Ford Granada car which had overtaken and braked hard in front of it. Then the van was rammed from behind by a small Ford van and hemmed in by another car.

The three security guards were surrounded by the armed raiders, wearing crash helmets and masks.

Shots were fired at the van's tyres to immobilize it and the radio was also put out of action to prevent the guards summoning help.

The security men were unhurt, although shaken.

The chain saw quickly cut an 18in square hole in the side of the van. The gang grabbed 35 bags containing £750,000, but overlooked another four containing £100,000. They fled on foot into woods and common land bordering Sutton Lane and were believed to have escaped in three cars parked in the district.

Last night detectives from Scotland Yard's newly formed central robbery squad, under the leadership of Detective Chief Superintendent James Sewell, travelled to Banstead. Mr Sewell said: "It was well planned. There must have been lots of eye-witnesses who were delayed at the scene while the raid was going on and we appeal for them to contact us."

Scotland Yard said: "Motorists must have thought there was some sort of accident. Obviously the thieves did not want members of the public to see what was going on. It was all over in a few minutes, so nobody became suspicious."

The raid was similar to another power-saw attack on a security van last December in Hertfordshire. Six armed men sliced through quarter-inch armour plate in a few seconds and stole £250,000 on that occasion.

The saw, which was dumped near the scene, had a 12-inch wide carbonite wheel and was operated by a pull-start petrol motor. A man was later arrested and jailed for the raid.

4 The next two versions are shorter than the previous ones. Are they detailed enough for you to form a clear picture of what happened?
(a) Which details are missing from A and B in these versions?
(b) Are there any additional pieces of information that emerge in these versions? If so, add them to your notes.
(c) Version C opens with a comparison of the security van to a sardine can. Does this help you to imagine what happened? Compare this with the description in the paragraph of B.

C

A POWER-SAW gang escaped with £750,000 yesterday after ripping open a security van like a sardine can.

But the four-minute ambush was so swift they missed bags containing another £100,000.

The Security Express van was rammed by a stolen car in Sutton Lane, Banstead, Surrey.

The gang of 10, wearing masks, goggles and crash helmets, leaped out of other vehicles.

They whooped as they charged the armoured van, which had two guards in the front and one locked in the back.

Two raiders opened fire with shotguns to shatter the windscreen and blow up a tyre.

A third shot put the van's emergency radio out of action.

A power saw was used to cut open the side of the van—and of the safe inside.

While the security guards were held at gun-point the raiders passed back 35 bags containing £750,000.

Some of the gang drove off with the haul in four or five getaway cars. Others fled through the grounds of a hospital.

Eye witness Mr David Gannie, on his way to his home in Sutton Lane, said the gang blocked the road with two cars taken from a car park opposite the ambush spot.

D

BANDITS armed with shotguns and a chain saw snatched £700,000 in a daring ambush on a security van yesterday.

The masked ten-man gang staged an accident to force the Security Express van to stop.

One of the gang lay in the road pretending to be injured. Another, in uniform, was directing traffic. As the van slowed down, it was surrounded and rammed by four cars.

The raiders raced to the truck and blasted the windows with gunfire.

They ordered the two guards to stay put — and shot out the radio to stop them calling for help. Then two of the gang used a chain saw to hack through the side of the truck.

They hauled the cash — in 35 sacks — into a black Ford Granada saloon.

The lightning raid in Sutton Lane, Banstead, Surrey, took just eight minutes. And in their haste the gang left behind five sacks containing £100,000.

Both security guards were unhurt.

Detective Chief Superintendent Jim Sewell, head of Scotland Yard's new Robbery Squad, said:

"This was a well-planned operation. A real professional job."

E **WITH chilling professionalism, an armed gang ambushed a security van, sliced it open with a power saw, and stole £750,000 yesterday.**

The operation, in a leafy lane, took precisely four minutes.

While it was going on, one of the gang posed as a policeman in a fluorescent jacket printed with the words 'POLICE. SLOW' to hold up traffic.

David Gammie, 26, who was on his way home along Sutton Lane, on the outskirts of Banstead, Surrey, said : 'The whole thing was made to look like an accident—they even had a person lying in the road pretending to be injured.'

The operation began at 1.35 p.m. as the yellow Security Express armoured van, carrying cash for local banks, drove north along the lane, bordered by hedges and common land.

Shotguns

As it came level with a bridle path, a pale blue Ford Granada overtook and cut in sharply, forcing the van to stop.

A blue Ford van rammed the Security Express van from behind and another car, a silver-blue Ford Escort blocked the bridle path.

Men wearing masks, crash helmets, and dark glasses and armed with sawn-off shotguns surrounded the security van.

They shot out two of its tyres, then the windscreen—and then its radio link with Security Express headquarters.

The three guards were warned not to move and, within seconds, a man with a power saw cut a 2ft. by 3ft. hole in the double metal 'skin' just behind the driver's door.

Meanwhile, down the lane in the direction of Banstead village, the bogus policeman was holding up the traffic. The gang removed 35 cash bags from the security van and loaded them into a Sherpa van.

Then, after four minutes, leaving four bags with £80,000 still in the security van, they all leaped into the Sherpa. It roared off along a tiny road through the grounds of Banstead Hospital.

On the other side, the gang drove along The Grange before stopping opposite Greenacre School, abandoning the van, and switching to two large saloon cars.

Motor

But not everything went according to plan. In the excitement of the getaway one of the gang's shotguns went off—accidentally, police think.

Before the ambush, the gang had gathered in good time in the parking area of Banstead Woods. People picnicking in the woods paid no attention—but they did when a total of seven vehicles drove off in convoy.

Detective Chief Superintendent Jim Sewell, head of Scotland Yard's robbery squad, said : 'This was a well organised, totally professional raid —these boys knew exactly what they were doing, even if the use of a power saw is unorthodox.'

It is believed that eight men were involved.

Detectives were checking the files on a similar raid on the M1 nine months ago, when six men, again using a power saw, got away with £250,000.

Only two of that gang were caught—and eventually jailed.

The saw used then had a 12in. wide sharpened carbonite wheel, which can bite through metal of almost any thickness, and was powered by a petrol motor started by a pull cord.

Workmen

A possible clue to yesterday's raid came from retired Mr Ernest Garmen, of Elgin Road, Sutton, who walks every day in Sutton Lane, scene of the robbery.

About a week ago he saw a group of men in blue boiler suits looking around the area —and a blue Ford Escort was parked nearby.

'I wondered if they might be council workmen,' he said.

It looked as though yesterday's ambush had set a record. Police said they could not remember a greater haul from a security van.

But the haul still does not compare with that of the Great Train Robbers—who 15 years ago, on August 8, 1963, stole £2½ million from a night mail train.

4

It was the middle of the night when my uncle woke me up and told me to climb a tree. I thought he was playing a joke on me, though he's not a person who plays jokes. In fact, he's usually a rather gloomy man and he thinks climbing trees is a waste of time, unless it's to pick coconuts or betelnuts or something useful.

My favourite climbing tree is the big branchy one with the thick trunk that stands near our house. (I mean, it used to stand there. I still can't get used to the idea that it's gone.)

When Uncle woke me it was very dark and I could hear the wind blowing hard and roaring in the branches of the tree. He hurried me outside and I couldn't even see the stars, so the sky must have been covered with clouds. It seemed an odd time to be climbing trees and I started to ask questions, but Uncle told me not to argue and to get climbing.

I knew the best way up with my eyes shut. I felt for the low branch above my head, pulled myself up until I could hook my legs over it and hoisted myself up and on to it. I called to Uncle that I was up, and he shouted, 'Higher! Higher!' I felt for the branches and stumps that I knew and climbed upwards until I was clinging to a thin branch that was tossing and swaying and seemed to be doing its best to throw me off.

The grownups were arguing in the darkness below. My uncle was trying to persuade my aunts and cousins to climb up too. I really thought he'd gone crazy like the man in the village the other side of the island who sometimes sits in the trees like a monkey. (I mean he used to, he's not there any more.) Uncle kept shouting, 'The water's coming! The water's coming!' Of course he was right, it did come. I don't know how he knew.

Above the noise of the wind in the branches I could hear some of the words of the argument going on below me. Uncle was shouting, 'Up the tree!' Other voices were saying 'Not that one', or 'To the boats! To the boats!' I shouted down, 'Come on, I'll help you!' But of course none of them could climb as well as me: they were either too old or too young. I don't think any of them got into my tree.

The wind tore at me and the branches thrashed about me but I was beginning to see things better. It was still nearly pitch dark but suddenly there was something darker and blacker flying through the air like a huge bat and wrapping itself round the lower branches of my tree. I heard the women's voices wailing, 'The roof! The roof!', and I knew it was the thatch of our house going to pieces. I'd seen this happen before. Roofs blow off quite often in the islands. And quite often the water comes up nearly to the top of the mound on which our house is built. But we'd never climbed trees in the middle of the night before.

When the water came it was different from other times. I could hear a roaring of water approaching even above the noise of the wind in the trees and then suddenly it was rushing around the trunk of the tree and pouring over the lower branches. I mean, it didn't rise slowly like the other floods I'd seen; it was halfway up the trunk all at once and I was wet with spray in the highest branches. And then the whole tree seemed to be moving. Yes, I know the branches had been moving but now I had the feeling that everything was slowly toppling, and then I was in the water though I was still holding the branch. And now it was the water instead of the wind that was trying to tear me off the branch, and the rough bark was hurting the skin on my chest and arms as I clung for my life. I struggled and reached for branches above me, caught one and pulled myself clear of the water. There were great salt waves washing over the tree. I could taste them and my eyes stung as I tried to climb above them. The tree was lying right over on its side, and climbing it was quite different. I reached a branch that was clear of the waves and clung on with my arms and legs.

The water didn't seem to be rushing round the trunk as it had been and in the darkness the tops of the other trees seemed to be moving away. Then I knew I was afloat, and alone in the darkness and the storm.

How should I know how long I floated, or how far? All I knew was that I must hang on. Though the current didn't drag at the tree, now that we were floating along with it, the wind still tugged at me and the spray broke over me. The night seemed without end. I even thought that perhaps the sun had been washed away too and it would never return.

I don't know how I got the feeling that I was always moving through the water, voyaging like a ship through the night. I can only remember the darkness of the sky and the blacker darkness of the waves, but perhaps I did see solid things that stayed still while I moved past them. They must have been the tops of palm trees that were still hanging on to the earth with their roots while the water swirled around them.

Then I think I remember feeling I must be dead or that everything had come to an end, because the wind died down and the waves stopped tearing at me and when I looked up I saw the stars. But all around me was darkness and water and all I could do was lie exhausted on my branch. I was nowhere and there was nothing I could do.

And then it all started again. I thought: *no, there can't be more of it; I can't go on.* But the wind was soon raging again and the waves were once again snatching at me. And somehow I did hold on, though there didn't seem to be any reason why I should. But I must have had enough of my wits about me to notice that I seemed to be going back the way I had come. Perhaps I saw those same palm-tree tops passing the other way – but no, I don't know where I got the feeling that I'd turned round and gone back. Now that I come to think of it, perhaps I never did. But I had this very strong feeling at the time.

By then I suppose I had no hope that the storm would ever stop or that things would ever be different. But now there came a change in the movement of the tree. Instead of drifting smoothly like a boat, it was bumping and lurching, and I remember thinking: *we've gone aground.* We stuck fast, and now the current was rushing past again, though the wind and waves were not so fierce. And it wasn't so dark. There was the glow in the sky you see before sunrise. Perhaps there was a sun after all!

I think the sun rose, the water drained away and the wind dropped all about the same time. And there I was.

Where? I was in the tree. The tree was lying on its side among mud and puddles. I had this feeling I was back where I had started, though nothing I could see as the light got stronger looked like the home I knew.

It was a land of mud and battered trees. There was a mound and a creek, but there were no houses on the mound and no boats in the creek. Yet if there *had* been houses on the mound, boats in the creek, more trees here and there and more branches on the trees that were standing, it could have been home.

---

1 What have we found out so far about:
(a) the person telling this story;
(b) where this person lives;
(c) what has happened?
2 Why does the person telling the story think that he or she is alone?
3 Can you find any further clues to the answers to these questions in the passage that follows?

I don't remember doing it, but I must have staggered across to one of the mounds and fallen asleep there. How long did I sleep? I don't know – hours, days, what does it matter? I remember slowly waking up, lying there with my eyes shut, thinking: *I've had a terrible dream, but when I open my eyes I shall see the houses and my family and the cows and the boats as usual.*

I opened my eyes. The dream was real. A warm winter sun was shining, and steam was rising from the muddy, empty fields. There lay my tree, and there were the tracks my feet had left as I walked away from it. There were no other tracks of men, animals or birds.

Around me stood battered trees that had more or less survived the storm: branching trees with their top branches wrenched off and all their leaves stripped; ragged palm trees, some of them leaning over until they nearly touched the earth. There were holes in the ground, full of water, where trees had been uprooted and carried away. Further off were the paddy fields where the rice plants lay plastered with mud. There was the empty creek, and beyond it the water of the great river running to the sea, sparkling happily in the sun.

I was lying on a pile of branches and palm leaves on a mound on which the houses must have stood. But the only sign of them was a few bits of palm matting tangled in the branches. And the only sounds were the clicking and snapping of things as they dried in the sun and the murmur of the water as it flowed past the shore. No human voices, no sounds of animals or birds.

I knew I was alive because I was thirsty. I thought there ought to be a well somewhere around, but I couldn't find it. Either I looked in the wrong place or it had got completely choked up with mud and rubbish. So I went down to the shore.

Well, you can't die of thirst on our islands. You can't always drink the water, of course. When the tide brings the sea water in from the bay you can't drink it, it's too salty. But at the end of the ebb tide it's the river water running past. It's not so clean that you can actually see through it, and I sometimes think it tastes of all the countries and towns it has flowed through, but you can drink it.

After I had drunk I looked out over the water and saw it was full of people. I knew they were dead, of course, and they were too far from the shore for me to see whether they were people I knew. There was nothing I could do for them.

I walked back to the mound again and sat down. My mind was empty as the island. I had to tell myself who I was. This is what I said to myself:

My name is Apu. Or perhaps that's not my proper name but it's what people call me. The name of my island is Kukuri Mukuri Char. I live there with my uncle Ahmed and my aunties and cousins. My father's name was Bashir but I don't remember him or my mother because they both disappeared in a boat in a storm soon after I was born. That's what my uncles and aunts always told me. Of course they had to bring me up.

That's all there was to know about me then. Perhaps I was always a little bit different from my cousins because I didn't actually have a father or mother. Perhaps I was a bit more used to looking after myself. Anyway I had to now.

Now I was hungry. The first thing I thought about was the paddy. The rice crop. You can't live without rice, can you? I went to the fields to look at it. Already the plants were beginning to straighten themselves up from the mud, but they didn't look as green and healthy as they should. The grains were not quite ripe but they hadn't fallen off. My uncles would have known whether they were all right or not, and if there was anything that could be done for them. I thought I could pick myself some rice and cook it. Then I remembered that I had no cooking pot, and no fire.

I wandered back to the mound, thinking there must be something left of the kitchen things. But there was nothing, not even a knife. I supposed all the pots had gone floating away on the water but I couldn't understand how the metal things had gone too. They may have just got buried in the mud somewhere, but I never found them. And anyway, how could I light a fire? Usually on the islands we keep a fire going all the time, but if it goes out we have these little sticks with black heads that make fire.

Oh, you know about matches? Well, I didn't have any matches.

In the end I found some roots to eat. You don't eat roots? We do; we sow the seeds in the ground and when the roots grow we eat them. They're better when they're cooked of course but you can eat them without cooking. I found some quite easily near the mound. The leaves were spoiled by the salt water but the roots were all right in the ground. I dug a few up with my fingers and wiped them and ate them.

So there I was with water and food, and sunshine, and the *lungi* I was wearing when I climbed the tree. You don't know what a *lungi* is? Well, it's just a tube of cloth, and you put your legs in and tie it round your middle. Mine

14

was pretty old, and it had got torn in the tree, but it was enough. You don't need much to keep you alive, do you?

It was winter so I didn't expect it would rain any more –

Oh, you think that sounds funny? It hardly ever rains in our winter. The sky's usually blue and the sun's warm in the daytime. It can be cold at night and it's good to have a fire and a blanket and a roof to protect you from the dew. So I thought I'd better make myself some kind of house. I collected some broken bits of matting from the branches and propped them against the base of a tree. I dried some straw in the sun and made myself a sort of nest to keep me warm.

And so the days passed. How many? It's funny the way people ask me that. I just didn't count the days. Why should I?

---

4 Imagine that you are a reporter for a TV or radio station. You have read the account printed above and want to interview the person telling the story to find out more about what happened, and how he or she has escaped. What questions would you ask? Make a list of them.
Are any of your questions answered in what follows? Read on, and find out:

The only thing that happened during this time was that aeroplanes flew overhead.

Oh, I'm not an ignorant savage, I know about aeroplanes. Nearly every day you used to be able to see one or two over the islands: shining ones that passed very high and straight, sometimes drawing white lines across the blue sky; fast ones that roared overhead, lower down; winking red lights at night. On the clear nights of winter we'd often see something that looked like a bright star sailing across the sky from one horizon to the other. The older men in the village said they'd never seen such things when they were young and that it was something people had made. But can people make stars?

I had a little cousin who used to wave at aeroplanes. But then she used to cry for the moon when she was younger. I knew that sort of thing was just childish. Even if all those aeroplanes had people in them, as I'd been told, it wasn't likely that they'd take any notice of us down there in the islands. And it was no use

thinking of reaching for the moon either.

At least, that's what I always thought until the aeroplane came to our island.

I was sitting in the sun, and if I had a thought in my head at all it was to wonder why there weren't even any birds about. I suppose they'd all just been blown away. It was this speck in the sky that made me start thinking about birds, and then the sound of its engine told me it wasn't a bird, but a machine. It made a rather rough, chopping sound as it came over the treetops, quite low down and quite slowly. The noise became louder and louder and then the aeroplane stopped still in the sky, nearly above me. I didn't know they could do that, though we do have some birds that can.

I thought this thing had great wings flapping above it, but as it hung there I could see they were spinning rather than flapping. It began to come down on me and a great wind came from it that clattered the palm leaves and raised the dust and dead leaves in clouds.

I was frightened. Not so much of the machine as by the wind it made. I had a good reason to be frightened of wind. I ran from the mound, across the paddy field, and hid in the first muddy ditch that I came to. The wind from the machine blew dust and paddy straw over my head.

The noise from the engine stopped. I lifted my head and peered towards it. It was standing among the paddy on four legs and it looked like a glass bottle with four drooping wings above it. I told myself I must be brave and go up to it – anyway, I thought, if it was looking for me it would easily find me.

I crawled out of the ditch and walked towards it, though my legs felt weak under me. As I did so a door opened in the glass bottle and some men got out.

Two of them at least were not like ordinary men. I thought they were looking at me with great metal eyes. Then I thought: *no, they are guns, they have come to kill me.* I was a simple village boy then, you see; I wasn't very sure about foreign men with hair like jute, or about the difference between a gun and a camera. I think I'd seen a man kill a duck with a gun, so I was afraid of these shining things pointed towards me. But there was no loud noise and

15

nothing happened.

The third man, who had black hair like myself, spoke to me in my own language – well, not quite the way we talk in the islands but I could understand what he meant. He asked me questions. The first question was: 'What is the name of the island?'

I said, 'I am not certain. Is it Kukuri Mukuri Char?'

I could see he pitied me and thought me a very ignorant boy, not even knowing the name of the island I was on.

The next question was: 'What is your name?' I was fairly sure about the answer to that one, so I told him.

Then he asked me who else lived on the island. I still don't know whether I gave the right answer to this question. I began by giving him the name of my uncle Ahmed, and the names of all my other uncles and aunts and cousins, and of the neighbours across the creek. And then I told him about the village on the other side of the island, and told him as many names as I could remember, including the man who used to sit up in the tree. It made me feel better to talk about them like this, and I felt it couldn't be true that they'd all disappeared with the water.

The man spoke to the others in a way I couldn't understand and one of them seemed to be writing it all down on paper. Then he asked me a question that seemed so strange that I took a long time before I answered it. 'Do you need food?' he asked.

Did I need food? Was there a clever answer to this one? Who doesn't need food? I've never met anyone who didn't need food. So I thought it was safe to answer yes.

The next question was: 'Do you need clothes?' I thought this was even harder. Everybody needs food, but not everybody needs clothes. In the summer my little cousins used to run about naked, and so did the crazy man in the other village sometimes. But most people would say they needed at least one *lungi* to wrap round them, or even two – one to wash and one to wear. And I thought if I said I didn't need clothes he might even take mine away from me, so I answered yes.

He put the next question in a different way.

He said: 'Is there enough water?' I didn't think it polite to say it was a silly question. *Enough water?* We'd had more than enough. And there was enough water round the island to make it an island. So I said yes, there was enough water.

Then the jute-haired man smiled at me kindly and made me feel I had answered the questions correctly. He said something in his strange speech and the dark-haired man said to me, 'Don't worry. The world will hear of this.' And they got back into their machine again and the noise started and the wings began to spin again and blow the straw and dust about. And I was frightened of the wind it made and ran and hid in the ditch again. The aeroplane went up into the air and moved quickly away.

Then a thought came to me. *If I had asked the men for a box of matches, would they have given me one?* But it was too late now.

The wind of the machine had blown away my roof of matting and my straw bed, and it took some time to gather it all up again. Then I gave myself a supper of cold radish and settled down for another lonely night with the saying in my head: 'The world will hear of this.' What could it mean? Had I done right or wrong?

---

5 Working in pairs, imagine that one of you is the pilot of the plane reporting back to base, and the other is the commanding officer speaking to the pilot by radio.

Make up what you think the pilot would say over the radio to his commanding officer, and the questions that the commanding officer would ask in order to find out the details of what the pilot has discovered.

Use only information you can find in the passages you have read so far to provide the pilot's answers to the commanding officer's questions.

6 What you have read so far is the opening of a story by Clive King called *The Night The Water Came*. Instead of dividing the story into chapters, the author has called each section of his story a *Tape*, because he imagines that the words have been spoken into a tape recorder by the person telling the story of what has happened. Tape 1 has this title:

Cyclone Strikes Islands

What is a cyclone? If the word is unfamiliar to you, you can still work out what it means by thinking about what you have read. From your reading,

what have you been told about what a cylone is and does? Refer to details in what you have read that provide the clues.
7 Tape 1 ends at the gap after 'it could have been home' on page 13. The remainder of what you have read is Tape 2. If you were the author, what title would you give for this Tape?
8 Tape 3, which is not reprinted here, has this title:

Airdrop

What does this mean?
Imagine you are Apu, the person telling the story. Imagine you are now making Tape 3. Tell the story of what happened as Apu would tell the story, describing the airdrop and how you reacted to it.
(a) Compare your version of Apu's third tape with that made by the person sitting next to you.
9 You will find out if you were right in your account of how Apu would have reacted to the airdrop if you read Tape 4 carefully:

You do get tired of living on roots and water. I felt a longing for fish, and if I'd had a net I could have tried to catch some. But of course I still had nothing to cook them with and raw fish is worse than raw roots.

I used to sit on the bank looking out over the water. Usually you can see a lot of fishing boats from our island but they, too, seemed to have vanished. I really thought at that time that, apart from the aeroplanes that stay in the sky, all the world had been drowned. An old aunt used to tell me a story of how this had happened once and I supposed it could have happened again.

But one day I saw a boat far out towards the open sea. No, it was two boats, three boats! So not all the fishermen had disappeared. They were moving very fast though, not the way our country boats move when the boatmen paddle them or punt them with long bamboos or sail them under their square sails. Then I heard a sound of engines and I thought: *an aeroplane, too.* I looked up into the sky, but there was nothing. The noise was coming from the boats. Oh yes, I'd seen motorboats, though I can't remember one ever coming to our island and actually stopping.

The boats came along: one, two, three, like ducks in a line. When they came nearer I could see that they didn't look like our country boats

at all. They didn't have the long curved beaks and sterns our boats have, nor houses on them. They looked like square boxes floating.

They came in from the sea, following the channel of deep water that I knew ran close to the shore of our island. There was a man standing up in the first boat pointing a pair of big glass eyes at me. They flashed in the sun. The man waved his arm and all three boats suddenly turned and came straight towards the shore where I was standing. I could see a number of big men standing in each of the boats, all dressed the same in mud-coloured clothes, and something put into my head the word: soldiers.

I'd never seen soldiers, only heard about them, but I felt afraid again. I thought: *they've come to fight, or take me prisoner.* Wasn't that what soldiers did? So I ran away.

It's difficult to hide on our island. I ran until I came to a ditch, and crouched down in it. When I peeped out through a clump of reeds I could see the enemy spreading out in a long line and walking towards me over the paddy fields. I could see that things weren't too easy for them either. Every now and then they would come to a ditch and they'd have to jump over it or wade through it. I ran along the side of my ditch, keeping my head down. I thought I might be able to get round the end of their line. When I looked up over the edge of the ditch again there was a soldier a few yards away. I think he was as startled as I was. I plunged through the ditch, over my knees in water and mud, and climbed out on the other side. The soldier shouted at me, but when I looked back he didn't seem to be in a hurry to get after me.

I ran and hid in a clump of trees around another *bari* mound, covering myself with fallen palm leaves. When I looked out again I could see the soldiers were still coming slowly after me, searching all the ditches and bushes as they came. They got nearer and I slipped out behind the mound and ran again. Again they shouted at me and came slowly on.

Although I wasn't feeling very strong after living on roots for all those days I felt I could have kept ahead of those soldiers if they hadn't cornered me on a point of land with the shore on one side and a big creek on the other. I

17

didn't feel strong enough to swim the creek so I just squatted there and let the soldiers come up to me.

Two of them stood and looked down at me, and I wondered what they would do. They both had pink faces and one of them had eyes the colour of the sky, which looked very strange. They said some words I didn't understand, then one of them took me by the arm. He was quite gentle about it but I thought: *now I'm a prisoner*.

There was a lot of blowing of whistles and shouting, and all the soldiers seemed to be gathering at my *bari* where I'd stacked the boxes. I knew they would soon find them and I supposed they would take them away with them. They led me back to my little house of boxes, and I wondered: *will they think I stole it all?* But they just looked at me and all the unopened boxes and seemed puzzled, not angry.

They made signs like eating, putting their hands to their mouths and pointing to the boxes. I couldn't understand what they wanted, then I thought: *perhaps they're hungry.* I searched among the straw of my bed and found a radish that I'd been keeping for supper, and offered it to them. I suppose one radish wasn't much among all those soldiers, though it was quite a lot to me. Some of them laughed, but some of them seemed almost to be crying.

Then one of them took a folding knife from his pocket and opened a little hooked blade. He dug this into one of the tins, cut the top off, and handed it to me. It had white sticky stuff inside it and I wasn't sure what to do with it, but the soldier put his finger into it and licked it, and I did the same.

It was the sweetest stuff I'd ever tasted, and after all those radishes of course it was delicious. They made me eat the whole tin.

Then I ran behind a tree and was sick.

After some more talk which I didn't understand, the soldiers led me towards the boats. I didn't want to be taken away from my home but I was too weak and sick to resist. The boats had square doors in the front that let down like flaps and they led me across one of these. The water had risen and the boats floated away quite easily. Then with a sudden roar that made me jump they started the engine. We went backwards away from the shore, turned together with the other boats and headed for the sea. I thought: *they're taking me far over the sea to a distant country and I shall never see my home again.* For the first time since the great storm, I cried.

10(a) Give a title for Tape 4.
(b) What impressions have you formed of the soldiers?
(c) What do you imagine they will do with Apu?
(d) How will Apu cope on arrival in 'the distant country'?

5

The pigeons flew out of the alley in one long swoop and settled on the awning of the grocery store. A dog ran out of the alley with a torn Cracker Jack box in his mouth. Then came the boy.

The boy was running hard and fast. He stopped at the sidewalk, looked both ways, saw that the street was deserted and kept going. The dog caught the boy's fear, and he started running with him.

The two of them ran together for a block. The dog's legs were so short he appeared to be on wheels. His Cracker Jack box was hitting the sidewalk. He kept glancing at the boy because he didn't know why they were running. The boy knew. He did not even notice the dog beside him or the trail of spilled Cracker Jacks behind.

Suddenly the boy slowed down, went up some steps and entered an apartment building. The dog stopped. He sensed that the danger had passed, but he stood for a moment at the bottom of the steps. Then he went back to eat the Cracker Jacks scattered on the sidewalk and to snarl at the pigeons who had flown down to get some.

Inside the building the boy was still running. He went up the stairs three at a time, stumbled, pulled himself up by the banister and kept going until he was safely inside his own apartment. Then he sagged against the door.

His mother was sitting on the sofa, going over some papers. The boy waited for her to look up and ask him what had happened. He thought she should be able to hear something was wrong just from the terrible way he was breathing. 'Mom,' he said.

'Just a minute. I've got to get these orders straight.' When she went over her cosmetic orders she had a dedicated, scientific look. He waited until she came to the end of the sheet.

'Mom.' Without looking up, she turned to the next page. He said again, *'Mom.'*

'I'm almost through. There's a mistake some –'

He said, 'Never mind.' He walked heavily through the living-room and into the hall. He threw himself down on the day bed.

His mother said, 'I'm almost through with this, Benjie.'

'I said, "Never mind".' He looked up at the ceiling. In a blur he saw a long cobweb hanging by the light fixture. A month ago he had climbed on a chair, written UNSAFE FOR PUBLIC SWINGING and drawn an arrow to the cobweb. It was still there.

He closed his eyes. He was breathing so hard his throat hurt.

'Benjie, come back,' his mother called. 'I'm through.'

'Never *mind*.'

'Come on, Benjie, I want to talk to you.'

He got up slowly and walked into the living-room. She had put her order books on the coffee table. 'Sit down. Tell me what's wrong.' He hesitated and then sat beside her on the sofa. She waited and then said again, 'What's wrong?'

---

1 What have you found out about the boy so far? Where does he live? Discuss your first impressions with the person sitting next to you.

2 Decide with your partner who will read the part of Benjie and who will read the part of his mother, then read the conversation between them as if it were a play:

Benjie: Mom
Mother: Just a minute. I've got to get these orders straight.
Benjie: Mom. (*pause*). Mom
Mother: I'm almost through. There's a mistake some ____

19

Benjie: Never mind.
Mother: I'm almost through with this, Benjie.
Benjie: I said 'Never mind'.
Mother: Benjie, come back. I'm through.
Benjie: Never *mind*.
Mother: Come on, Benjie, I want to talk to you. Sit down. Tell me what's wrong. (*pause*) What's wrong?

Pay close attention to the tone of voice in which you speak these lines. You will have to look back at the complete passage to find out how to say 'Never mind', for instance. The author gives no clues about the mood of Benjie (and so the way he speaks) in the words that have been left out when the conversation is set out like the script of a play.
3 Now read on. What else do you find out about Benjie?

He did not answer for a moment. He looked out of the window, and he could see the apartment across the street. A yellow cat was sitting in the window watching the pigeons. He said in a low voice, 'Some boys are going to kill me.'

'Not *kill* you, Benjie,' she said. 'No one is –'

He glanced quickly at her. 'Well, how do I know what they're going to do?' he said, suddenly angry. 'They're chasing me, that's all I know. When you see somebody chasing you, and when it's Marv Hammerman and Tony Lionni and a boy in a black sweat shirt you don't stop and say, "Now, what *exactly* are you guys planning to do – kill me or just break a few arms and legs"?'

'What did you do to these boys?'

'What did *I* do? I didn't do anything. You think I would do something to Marv Hammerman who is the biggest boy in my school? He is bigger than the eighth-graders. He should be in high school.'

'I know you did something. I can always tell. Now, what happened?'

'Nothing, Mom. I didn't do anything.' He looked down at his shoes. With his foot he began to kick at the rug. A little mound of red lint piled up in front of his tennis shoe.

'They wouldn't be after you for nothing.'

'Well, they are.' He paused. He knew he had to give an explanation, but he could not give the right one. He said, 'Maybe Hammerman just

doesn't like me. I don't know. I'm not a mind reader.'

'Look at me, Benjie.'

Without looking up he said, 'Mom, just listen to what Hammerman did to this boy in my room one time. This boy was in line in the cafeteria and Hammerman came up to him and –'

'What I want to hear is what happened *today*, Benjie.'

'Just *listen*. And this boy in the cafeteria was standing in line, Mom, doing absolutely nothing, and Hammerman comes up to him and –'

'Benjie, what happened *today*?'

He hesitated. He looked down at his tennis shoe. There was a frayed hole in the toe, and he had taken a ballpoint pen and written AIR VENT and drawn a little arrow pointing to the hole.

'What happened?' she asked again.

'Nothing.' He did not look at her.

'Benjie –'

'Nothing happened.'

She sighed, then abruptly she looked up. 'The beans!' She walked to the kitchen, and he lay back on the sofa and closed his eyes.

'Benjie?' He looked up. His mother was leaning around the door, looking at him. 'Why don't you watch television? Get your mind off yourself. That always helps me.'

'No, it won't help.'

'Well, let's just see what's on.' She came back in, turned on the television and waited for the set to warm up. He closed his eyes. He knew there was nothing on television that could interest him.

---

4 Read through the conversation between Benjie and his mother aloud with your partner. Again, use what the author tells us in the description of what they do to help you decide the tone of voice in which you speak. For instance,

'What happened?' she asked again.
'Nothing'. He did not look at her.
'Benjie _____'
'Nothing happened'.
She sighed, then abruptly she looked up. 'The beans!'

The words underlined give important clues to the way you say 'Nothing' and 'The beans!'

5 In the remainder of the passage, the author concentrates on a particular feature of Benjie's character. What is it? Have you seen any sign of this characteristic in the previous sections you have read?

'Tarzan!' his mother said. 'You always have loved Tarzan.'

He opened his eyes and glanced at the screen. In the depths of the jungle, a hunter had stumbled into quicksand, and Tarzan was swinging to the rescue.

'All the hunter has to do,' he said with a disgusted sigh, 'is lie down on the quicksand and not struggle and he won't sink.'

'That wouldn't leave anything for Tarzan to do though, would it?' his mother said, smiling a little.

'Oh, I don't know.' He closed his eyes and shifted on the sofa. After a minute he heard his mother go back into the kitchen. He opened his eyes. On the screen the hunter was still struggling. Cheetah was beginning to turn nervous somersaults. Tarzan was getting closer.

Once he and his friend Ezzie had made a list of all the ways they knew to stay alive. Ezzie had claimed he could stay alive in the jungle for ever. Ezzie said every jungle emergency had a simple solution.

Lying on the sofa, he tried to remember some of those old emergencies.

A second one came into his mind. Emergency Two – Attack by an Unfriendly Lion. Lion attack, Ezzie claimed, was an everyday occurrence in the jungle. What you had to do to survive was wait until the last moment, until the lion was upon you, and then you had to ram your arm all the way down the lion's throat. This would choke him and make him helpless. It was bound to be a little unpleasant, Ezzie admitted, to be up to your shoulder in lion, but that couldn't be helped.

'Is the Tarzan movie any good?' his mother asked from the kitchen.

'No.' He reached out with his foot and turned off the television. He sighed. Nothing could take his mind off Marv Hammerman for long.

'If it makes you feel any better,' his mother said, 'Teddy Roosevelt had the same problem. I saw it on television. Boys used to pick on him

and chase him.'

'No, it doesn't,' he said. He waited a minute and then asked, 'What did Teddy Roosevelt do about it?'

'Well, as I remember it, Teddy's father got him a gymnasium and Teddy exercised and got strong and nobody ever picked on him again.'

'Oh.'

'Of course, it wasn't the same as –'

'Don't bother getting me a gymnasium.'

'Now, Benjie, I didn't –'

'Unless you know of some exerciser that gives instant muscles.' He thought about it for a minute. He would go out, exerciser in his pocket, and say, 'Here I am, Hammerman.' Then, just when Hammerman was stepping towards him, he would whip out the exerciser, pump it once, and muscles would pop out all over his body like balloons.

'Well, you'll handle it,' his mother said. 'In a few weeks you'll look back on this and laugh.'

'Sure.'

He lay with his eyes closed, trying to remember some more of the old ways he and Ezzie knew to survive life's greatest emergencies.

Emergency Three – Unexpected Charge of an Enraged Bull. Bulls have a blind spot in the centre of their vision, so when being charged by a bull, you try to line yourself up with this blind spot.

'Fat people can't do it, Mouse,' Ezzie had told him. 'That's why you never see any fat bull-fighters. You and I can. We just turn sideways like this, see, get in the blind spot and wait.'

He could remember exactly how Ezzie had looked, waiting sideways in the blind spot of the imaginary bull. 'And there's one other thing,' Ezzie had added. 'It will probably work for a rhinoceros too.'

Emergency Four – Crocodile Attack. When attacked by a crocodile, prop a stick in its mouth and the crocodile is helpless.

At one time this had been his own favourite emergency. He had spent a lot of time dreaming of tricking crocodiles. He had imagined himself a tornado in the water, handing out the sticks like party favours. 'Take that and that and that!' The stunned crocodiles, mouths propped open, had dragged themselves away. For the rest of their lives they had avoided children with sticks in their hands. 'Hey, no!' his dream crocodiles had cried, 'Let that kid alone. He's got sticks, man, *sticks*!'

Abruptly he turned his head toward the sofa. The smile which had come to his face when he had remembered the crocodiles now faded. He pulled a thread in the slip cover. The material began to pucker, and he stopped pulling and smoothed it out. Then he took a pencil from his pocket and wrote in tiny letters on the wall PULL THREAD IN CASE OF BOREDOM and drew a little arrow to the sofa.

The words blurred suddenly, and he let the pencil drop behind the sofa. He lay back down. Hammerman was in his mind again, and he closed his eyes. He tried hard to think of the days when he and Ezzie had been ready to handle crocodiles and bulls, quicksand and lions. It seemed a long time ago.

6(a) What have you found out about (i) Ezzie; and (ii) how Benjie feels towards him?
(b) What do Benjie's thoughts about Tarzan and the Emergencies tell us about him?
(c) You can find out more about Benjie in the *Eighteenth Emergency* by Betsy Byars. What do you think the eighteenth emergency might be?

6

This passage is taken from a story by Ivan Southall. It is about a boy with a problem. As you read, think about what you find out about this boy and his feelings.

Well, he wouldn't be doing his stupid old project or his stupid old model, not even because he had said he would, not even to make Mum happy. They could rot; they could burst into flames. A plastic model of 227 pre-cut pieces stuck together with knobs and slots and dobs of glue, because he wasn't allowed to make a real model out of wood with knives and chisels; a project about stupid old cheese on a smudged piece of card (30 inches by 24 inches) with words and pictures cut from magazines.

'You know you can't print your own words properly because you can't hold a pen for any length of time without your hand shaking and going all silly, and you don't want to spoil your project, do you?'

Could he slip off into Sherbrooke Forest and find lyrebirds and wombats and wallabies and ant-eaters and possums?

Could he take his rod and fish in the Sassafras Creek on the way?

Could he dig a hole in the yard, a big deep hole like the other boys dug?

Like the big hole in Percy Mullen's backyard that was a smuggler's cave, a gold mine, a fortress, a volcanic crater, the Colosseum with the lions roaring for their tea. It had places in it for secret things. It was a club room. It was a real, beaut hole. In winter it filled with water and was then the Pacific Ocean, or the Bay of Bengal, or a sinking ship with all hands to the pumps. It was dangerous, too, and Mr Mullen was always going to fill it in, but he didn't.

Maybe Mr Mullen remembered that he had been a boy.

Could he climb on to the roof and sit on the ridge? The roof was always there like a mountain, like the Matterhorn, like an Everest, conquered by others but not by himself. Percy Mullen not only sat on roofs but jumped off them as well, but Percy was allowed to do almost anything, even chop down trees.

Sissy Parslow had sat on his roof. 'I'm the king of the castle,' Sissy had jeered, 'and you're the dirty rascal.'

Sissy was a creep.

John saw the flock of starlings come back (those starlings that had carried away his chains), all screeching and fluttering to alight on a telephone wire. First they looked like a string of brown beads; then like chattering children, bobbing and balancing, lined up for the race of their lives; but Mum had said she would use the telephone. 'I'll ring from Melbourne to see how you are, so don't go away.'

There was an arrow in the sky and it pierced the balloon. It fell back to earth clanking like a chain.

That wonderful feeling of calm and contentment and excitement, of being able to do as he pleased and not as other people said, turned over inside him like a page that was gone.

He couldn't go to the forest because he had to stay home.

He couldn't dig a hole because he wasn't allowed to use the tools.

He couldn't climb on to the roof because it would take too long to get down to the phone.

His mother's words, everyone's words, thudded over the top of him like traffic on a wooden bridge.

23

That horrid little telephone; that green monster was going to sit there all day like a big fat ear. For as long as he watched it it would brood; for as long as he thought about it it would threaten; as soon as he turned his back it would leap up and down screeching, 'Don't do this. Don't do that. Don't. Don't.' Then an hour later it would ring again.

That was why Mum had left it till last; so he couldn't argue; so he couldn't talk back. 'I'll ring you from Melbourne, so don't go away.' It was a real, grown-up, dirty trick.

'It's not fair,' he wailed, and in a flash of temper hurled a stone from the path straight down the drive and out through the arch of cherry-plum trees to frighten a whole day's growth out of Mamie van Senden.

Mamie was wearing blue jeans and a yellow jumper and golden hair like a polished brass helmet and was trotting bird-like along the road with a bag and a shopping list.

'Arr,' she shrieked and stopped dead, framed by the arch, and looked straight up the path, straight at John, then shrilled, 'Did you do that, John Sumner? What'd you do that for? You half-witted or something?'

'No, I'm not, I didn't know you were coming.'

'I'll bet you did.'

'I did not.'

'It's dangerous, throwing stones. I'll tell my Mum you're throwing stones. If I'd been riding my horse it would have bolted; then I'd have been killed and they'd have hung you for murder or something.'

'Serves you right for riding a horse. What do you want to be riding a horse along here for? You shouldn't ride one until you're big enough. You're too little.'

'You're only jealous 'cos you can't ride one yourself.'

'I can too. I can ride any horse I like. I can ride a brumby, I can ride a steer.'

'You're a real nut,' Mamie shrilled, and was about to shout something else but choked it back. Mamie had been told she was not to tease John Sumner about things he couldn't do, nor was she to play with him at all if she could avoid it in any way. It would be awful if he hurt himself and she got the blame. So she tossed her head and blushed and ran off along the road.

John blushed too, because Mamie was nice and he was sorry he had frightened her. He wished he could carry her bag home from school the way Percy Mullen carried Elspeth Winter's bag, but he didn't like to, because Mamie was little, only nine. One day when she was bigger he would invite Mamie to his birthday party and Mamie would come.

'Mamie,' he called, not very loudly, but she didn't answer, even when he hurried down to the arch and called again. 'Mamie van Senden!'

She was too far away, or didn't want to hear.

John sat under the arch on a white-painted stone. It was the Stone of Scone, though he didn't tell people about it because it was important that it should never be known that the Stone in Westminster Abbey was not the real one. Otherwise there'd be the devil to pay. Sometimes when he sat there he was King John and people passing by were scurvy barons hatching a plot to weaken the power of the throne. Sometimes he was the Archbishop of Canterbury having a rest between coronations because kings were dying so thick and fast he was plumb worn out from lifting crowns on to their heads.

Harry Hitchman came along on his bike, steering in curves round invisible obstacles. They were landmines and Harry knew if he brushed one with a wheel there would be a disaster. If one exploded it would trigger off the lot and the life of every person in the street depended on him.

'Hi, Harry.'

Harry went by, weaving expertly, concentrating ferociously.

Harry was as sure-footed as a mountain goat, even on a bicycle. He was also strong enough to hit a ball to the fence on the oval where the grown-ups played, and that took some doing for a twelve-year-old, though he wasn't very bright at school.

'Hi Harry.'

Harry was tall for his age. Harry could fight, too. Harry gave Sissy Parslow a terrible hiding one night after school. They had to take Sissy to the doctor to be stuck together again. It was murder, the kids said. John had been sad in a way but he loved Harry for it because Harry got into awful trouble and took all the blame himself. 'If that Sissy Parslow takes a poke at you again,' Harry had said to John, 'I'll let him have it next time, good and proper.'

'Hi, Harry.'

But Harry weaved away dodging land-mines. John was always a bit shy where Harry was concerned. He didn't like to raise his voice. He didn't want Harry to think he was a clinging vine.

Mrs Parslow drove by in her new Holden Premier. She was driving two hundred yards to the shops. (Main Street was the next road across.) She thought she was Lady Muck. The car was ivory and bronze with white side-walls. Sissy sat in front with a smug look on his face, with his nose turned up and his eyes directed ahead. He thought he was Christmas but he was a creep. His three horrible sisters sat in the back. They thought they were Princess Anne and hoped the neighbours were watching.

'It beats me where these people get the money from,' John's mother had said. 'Fred Parslow must have won it in a raffle.

Dad had replied, 'Don't be catty, dear, if we can run two cars, allow them one.'

'But you're a man of importance. Fred Parslow's a two-bit clerk.'

A little black ant carrying a big crumb came close to John's foot. He stopped every few inches to catch his breath, then heaved up his load and struggled on. In ten minutes he covered a yard. He was terrific. Then another little black ant hurried down to meet him. He dashed here and there in a state of high excitement but the first little ant stood beside his crumb with one foot raised in a threatening manner. 'Put your filthy paws on my crumb,' he screamed, 'and I'll knock you into the middle of next week. Find a crumb of your own.'

'Hi, Percy.'

Percy Mullen had a young Australian terrier on a lead. It was scarcely 9.45 but Percy already looked as though he had been dragged through a bush by the hair of his head. Percy always looked like that. The terrier was only knee-high to a grasshopper but was pulling fiercely on the lead and dashing to and fro, making horrible choking sounds. Percy had his hands full. 'You bloomin' little pest,' he wailed, 'what's wrong with you? Do you want to strangle yourself or somethin'?'

'Hi, Percy.'

'Hi, John.'

'Where you off to, Percy?'

'Search me,' panted Percy, and stumbled after the terrier.

'I'll come with you, Percy.'

'Little crumb,' Percy yelled at the terrier, 'you'll never die of old age, that's for sure.'

'Hey! Percy!'

The call was like a little kid with short legs who couldn't catch up.

The street was empty again. Percy wasn't there, Sissy Parslow wasn't there. Harry wasn't there. Mamie wasn't there. Neither was the ant.

The Giffords' car went past.

Mr Gifford was a shire councillor and most fearfully important. He came to the school on special occasions and spoke for half an hour. He was a fat man with white hair and purple cheeks and a nose like a heap of red gravel. He had a notice on his front fence, 'Trespassers will be shot'. Kids used to walk by on the other side in case a cannon popped out. Mum said the notice had been there for thirty years, for as long as she had lived in Wilson Street, anyway. Mr Gifford had never shot anyone – unless he buried all the bodies in secret or had come to a special agreement with Constable Baird about not getting arrested.

The grocer drove by.

'H-H-Hi, Mr Neal.'

Mr Neal must have been busy doing mental arithmetic adding up his profits.

---

7 How would you describe John's mood? Is it similar to Benjie's? Read through the passage again quickly, looking for any clues to the way he feels. Make a list of them, in brief note-form, then compare your list with your partner's.

8 How does he feel towards other people? Again, make a list in note-form. For instance,
   Sissy Parslow hates him: 'a creep', 'a smug look on his face' 'His three horrible sisters'.

9 There is one way in which John particularly resembles Benjie (see pages 19-22). How? Find two instances of this characteristic in what you have read so far.

10 Where does this boy live? Which words give us clues?

11(a) This chapter, and the story from which it is taken, is called *Let The Balloon Go*. There is a reference to a balloon early in the chapter:

> There was an arrow in the sky and it pierced the balloon. It fell back to earth clanking like a chain.

Why has the author called the story *Let The Balloon Go*, do you think?

There is a clue in the paragraph that follows the sentences quoted here.

(b) Do you find out anything you don't know already about John in the remainder of this passage?

The Stone of Scone suddenly got too hard. It usually did after a while. Even kings when they got crowned didn't have to sit on it for hours.

'Aw, h-heck,' John said, 'I'd b-b-better do my blooming old model.'

Then the explosion came.

Bang.

He felt like a billion bits blasting off in all directions.

'I'm not goin' back inside; I'm blooming well not.'

He didn't know that his hand was beating his thigh, that he was stammering aloud.

'I'm going to do what I want to do. I'll–I'll build a tree-house. That's what I'll do.'

The idea shocked him. It came so suddenly it could have dropped from the morning sky. John turned to run, but stumbled, and fell bewildered on the coarse gravel of the driveway.

He lay there stinging for several seconds before he moved (hurt more inside than outside), then discovered that he was trembling all over. 'Oh, golly,' he moaned, and shifted awkwardly to the grassy bank below the Stone of Scone. There, after a few tries, he managed with a shaking hand to dislodge the pieces of gravel that stuck to him. There was not much blood but he had skinned his knee-cap and grazed an elbow.

'It's not fair. Other kids don't fall.'

Mum would say, 'How did it happen? How could you possibly fall and hurt yourself like that? Weren't you making your model? Weren't you doing your project? Weren't you taking your nap? That's not a fall from standing up. That's a fall from running.'

Little by little he straightened his legs and tried to relax before the stupid old shakes had a chance to set in properly. He had got himself too excited; the grown-ups were always telling him not to, but what did they know about it? It was like telling a tree not to grow or a seed not to send up a shoot. And to make it worse he was at the roadside and everyone passing would see; old stickybeaks peering through curtains might spot him, even Mamie or Harry or Percy might come back, or creepy Sissy Parslow and his horrible sisters might leer at him from their car.

John pleaded with the shakes to go away. 'Not today. Please.'

A car was coming, too, just when he didn't want it, stopping and starting, with a door slamming, but the engine running all the time. It would have to be the baker and if the baker found him like this Mum would hear, she'd be told, and that would be the end of it; there would never be another day.

'I told you so,' Mum would say; 'didn't I tell you, John? What on earth must people think of me? Leaving you all alone.'

He crabbed along the grassy bank because if he stood up someone might see him; then when he was screened by the arch of cherry-plum trees he crawled into it a little way, but not too far because of the spikes on the branches. Perhaps he could have walked to the house, but he wasn't sure of himself, and for some reason it had become very important that not a soul should know. He didn't really worry about it over much at other times, but today it was a matter of pride. Today he wasn't the little spastic kid; today he was John Clement Sumner, the red-blooded boy who lived inside the one that shook and jerked and smudged his pages.

7

Here are two extracts from a novel by Susan Cooper called *Dawn of Fear*. As you come to spaces where words are missing, write down words that you think would fill the gaps and make sense.

The air-raid siren went at the beginning of the afternoon, in an English lesson, while Mrs Wilson was reading them 'Children of the New Forest'. At first they couldn't hear the siren at all for the school whistles; a chorus of alarm, their own indoor warning, shrilling down all the corridors at once.

'Ma'am, ma'am! A raid, ma'am!'

Mrs Wilson closed the book with a deliberate snap and stood up. 'All right now, children, quickly and quietly. Books in your desks, take out your gas masks, all stand up. Anybody not got his gas mask? Very good. Now I want a nice neat line to the shelter, and no running.'

A hand was waving wildly at the front of the class. 'Ma'am, is it a real raid, ma'am?'

'It's a drill,' said a scornful voice.

'It's the wrong time for a drill.'

Mrs Wilson scowled, and they knew the scowl and were quiet. 'We don't know yet. Door monitor?'

Little Albert Russell was already stiff at attention by the open door, the strap of his gas-mask case neat across his chest. Out they went into the corridor, from one row of desks at a time, their double file jostling the filing classes from the other rooms, out to the air-raid shelters in the playground.

Derek and Peter had desks near the classroom window. Geoffrey was behind them.

'Can you see anything?'

'Nah. Hear the siren now, though. Listen.'

The head-splitting school whistles had stopped, and Derek listened as he walked, and heard the distant wail of the siren rise and fall until they were down the corridor and going out of the big double door. He and Peter and Geoff were nearly at the end of the line; Mrs Wilson was counting heads just in front of them. He shivered; the sun was shining through broken clouds, but there was a chill wind. Most of the other classes, the younger ones, were made to take their overcoats into the shelters, but his group, the farthest from the cloakrooms, had no time ever to fetch theirs.

He became conscious suddenly of the drone of engines somewhere high up.

'Look!' Peter stopped, excited, pointing.

The three couples behind them fell over their feet as he stopped, and then skirted him and went nervously, disapprovingly on. Only Geoffrey paused. The girl who had been walking with him called over her shoulder, 'Come on,' but she was Susan Simmons, who was always bossy, and the boys took no notice, but stood where they were and stared up.

A

Where Peter was pointing, there was a pattern of slow-moving dots in the sky. The deep hum of the engines grew as he watched and developed a kind of throbbing sound. The clouds were very high, and the planes were flying below them; they seemed light-coloured and were not easy to see unless the sun went behind a cloud. Their noise seemed so loud now that Derek looked all around the rest of the sky for more, but saw nothing except the familiar floating shapes of the seven barrage balloons, three near, four far off, fat silver ovals hanging up there with bulbous fins at their tails, like great friendly bloated _____. The balloons were filled with hydrogen, he knew, and _____ by thick cables; they were there to get in the way of any Nazi pilot coming in low to drop his bombs.

'Junkers,' Geoffrey said confidently. 'Junker eighty-eights.'

What with his own excitement and the height of the formation, Derek could not really make out the _____ of any individual plane; but by the same _____ he knew that Geoff couldn't either. 'No, no,' he said. 'Dorniers'.

And then in the second that they still _____ on the black asphalt playground, with the grubby concrete boxes that were the air-raid shelters looming ahead of them, they saw the unbelievable happen. Suddenly the rigid, steadily advancing formation of enemy planes broke its _____ lost its head as plane after plane broke away and _____ and they heard a new higher noise and glimpsed, diving through a broad gap in the clouds out of the sun, a _____ of other smaller _____ planes _____ the bombers as a dog scatters sheep. It was a _____ sky now, full of _____ ing gunfire.

They heard other guns open up, deeper, closer, on the ground.

B

'Gosh!' Derek said. He had forgotten entirely where he was; he hopped in delight. His gas-mask case banged at his back. 'Gosh!'

'Fighters, our fighters!' Peter waved madly at the sky. 'Look!'

And they were lost in breathless looking and in the growing _____ of engines and the _____ ing of gunfire, as an _____ hand came down and Mrs Wilson dragged them off towards the shelter.

'You stupid boys, come under cover at once!' Her voice was a _____ of anxious rage, and it was only the realization that she was angrier than they had ever seen her that brought them _____ ing into the entrance of the shelter. But even then Peter was still _____ back over his shoulder, and all at once he let out a yell of such joyful surprise that all four of them, even Mrs Wilson, paused, _____ , for a last _____ of the sky.

'He's got him, he's got him, he's got him!'

C

It was a Hurricane – Derek could see the blunt nose now – and it had dived after one of the weaving bombers, with its guns making bright _____ on its wings. And the bomber had been hit; it was _____ a ragged path of black smoke behind it and _____ ing erratically across the sky and down. It was still firing its guns; you could hear them and see them among the _____ of smoke in the sky that were the burst of shells fired from the ground. Nearer and nearer the ground the plane came, a long way away from them but still _____ and as it dived, it _____ close to one of the motionless silver barrage balloons, and suddenly there was a sound like a soft 'whoomph' and a great _____ of flame.

The plane dropped and vanished, with the victorious Hurricane above it _____ off to join the battle that they could still hear but no longer see; the sound of the crash was no more than a faraway thump, like the firing of one of the anti-aircraft guns, but enough to _____ Mrs Wilson into thrusting them ahead of her around the right-angle bend of the entrance into the shelter itself. But still Derek had one moment's last quick sight over his shoulder of the burning barrage balloon, hanging there in the sky as it always had but beginning strangely to _____ with its fat inflated fins no longer sticking firmly out but curving gently, wearily, down.

When they came out of the shelter about half an hour later, the barrage balloon was no longer there. Instead, there was a gap in the sky and only six floating guardian shapes. The raid had not lasted for very long; there had been time for a handful of songs – the other three classes of children in their shelters had been singing 'Waltzing Matilda' when they came in – and the distribution of one boiled sweet each. Then the noise outside, which they heard only in the brief gap between one song and the next, had died away, and the long single note of the 'all clear' had shrilled out. They went back to their classrooms, in as neat a double file as before, and bossy Susan Simmons made a shocked face at Derek and Peter and Geoff and whispered to her friends as they passed.

The three boys stayed after school, hovering at

their desks until everyone else had left, to apologize to Mrs Wilson, and curiously she did no more than give them a brief lecture on the perils of being out in the open when a raid was on, and the undeniable extra crime of giving someone else the risk of coming to haul them inside.

'She's nice,' Derek said on the way home. 'I mean, she could have sent us to the Head, and then they'd have told our parents, and there'd have been an awful row.'

'She ought to be grateful, if you ask me,' Peter said. 'If she hadn't had to come and find us, she'd have missed all the fun.'

Struggling into sweater and shoes and dressing-gown, Derek felt empty and sick with fear of the night and the noises it was making. He was still heavy with sleep, but the fear was there, very strong and unfamiliar, and he did not know how to handle it. As they went quickly out into the darkness, he held tightly to his mother's hand and looked up and saw the white criss-crossing arms of the searchlights sweeping the black sky, and small and far off the bursting stars of shells, and below and behind it all the red glow to the eastern sky, as if he were seeing them all for the first time.

D

In the small, dank, earth-smelling box of the shelter, it was better at first, because they were all close together. Even though the noise outside grew steadily worse, Derek lay curled and _____ and almost fell asleep. But at the pit of his stomach the fear still _____ . And all at once it jabbed him viciously as the roar of a diving plane _____ out of the dull background of rumbling and thumps, and while it still filled his head, there were two great crashes somewhere close. He felt his bunk _____ and he _____ upright and hit his head on the roof. He had a glimpse of his father's face, strained and _____ .

Then the third explosion came, and it was as if the world had blown up. The noise _____ through his head so that it _____ in his ears even after he knew that it had stopped. He ducked automatically and stayed crouched with his head on his knees. He had never heard anything so shatteringly loud. His bunk and the whole shelter _____ and shook, and outside in the night

there was a sequence of other smaller, closer noises, noises of breaking and clattering and something that sounded like tiles falling from their own roof. The shelter gave a second _____ much fainter than the first, and then the worst close noise was gone, and there was only the _____ rumbling again and the sound of the guns, and Derek raised his head _____ ly and stared at his mother and father in the dim light of the _____ ing candle flame. His mother reached up and took hold of his arm and held it tightly. 'All right, love. All right.' Blanket-bundled in her arms, Hugh whimpered, and she bent her head to murmur to him.

John Brand moved to the candle and pinched out its flame between his finger and thumb, then warily pulled the black-out curtain and the wooden cover over the shelter entrance a little way aside. Derek peered out at what little of the gap he could see, and gasped. The night was not dark now. It was a dusky red, and its light was strangely flickering.

His father turned back. He rattled a box of matches and gave it to Mrs Brand, still holding the entrance open with one hand.

'Down the road,' he said. 'Looks like a direct hit. I shall have to go and help, love.'

'Oh, John –'Mrs Brand said, and her voice was shallow and quavering as Derek had never heard it before.

'Look,' John Brand said. 'It must have been the one plane. Off course from the factories, like last time. There's nothing else coming down. Not now.'

'You don't know,' she said.

'It might have been us,' he said. 'Thank God it wasn't. They need help. I'll be back as soon as I can.' He kissed her quickly. 'Stay down until the all-clear goes.' He pressed Derek's knee hard. 'Look after them, Derry,' he said.

'Be careful,' Mrs Brand said softly.

He went out, and Derek heard the rattle of the wooden cover going back into place, and his father was gone.

His mother laid Hugh gently on the bunk, checked the blackout, and lit the candle again.

Derek said suddenly, his voice coming out high and hoarse, 'Dad isn't going to get shot, is he, Mum?'

'Of course not, love,' she said, and reached up

and hugged him. 'He'll be very careful. But one of the houses down the road was hit by that last bomb. Daddy could see the fire. So everyone has to go and get the people out of the house before they get hurt.'

The guns were still thumping, but the rumble of planes had died away. Derek looked at the candle flame, sending up its quivering black line of smoke, and lay back on his bunk. 'Peter's dad will be helping, too,' he said. 'And Geoff's. They live closer to that end than we do. I expect Pete's dad was the first there. Whose house do you think it was, Mum? Old Mr Graham at the end of the road?'

'I don't know, love,' she said. 'But I hope no one was hurt. Now you try to get some rest until the all-clear goes. Hughie's asleep; we don't want to wake him up.'

Derek thought: 'The guns are still making as much noise as our talking is.' But all the same he knew what his mother meant. People's voices were not usual, but small Hugh was used to the talking of the guns. They were a normal background to his sleep, every night.

His father had not come home when the all-clear sounded. The sky was beginning to lighten with the dawn, and somewhere a single bird had begun to chirrup. Derek helped his mother back into the house with Hugh; then drank some cocoa with her in the kitchen, feeling strange and adult and unreal. Flames were still flickering down the road, and it did look as though they were coming from the Grahams' house. Old Mr Graham was the sort of man to whom one always said good morning politely; he was thin and white-haired, but very upright, with a neat waxed moustache. He lived three doors away from the Hutchinses, and he had a plump and smiling wife whom they seldom saw. Derek wondered what they would do without their house. He thought: 'Pete must have a good view.'

Then he went dutifully to bed leaving Mrs Brand waiting in the kitchen, and his determination to stay awake dissolved as soon as he lay down and pulled up the bed-clothes and felt his mother slip into the room and tuck him in. He fell asleep, and this time did not dream.

1 Look back through the passages where words are missing and compare your suggestions with those of other members of your class or group: How many different words could fill the gaps and make sense? Which do you prefer?

2(a) How has Derek changed in the way he feels about the air raids?

Compare his attitude in the opening extract with the way he feels after the second attack.

(b) Which words tell us how he feels?

(c) Can you suggest why the author has called the novel *Dawn of Fear*?

3 Compare your choice of words to complete the gaps with the words listed (in alphabetical order) on p. 44. Where the author's words differ from yours, think about how their meanings are different also.

8

1 From reading this Prologue, what do you think the story will be about? Are there any clues?

PROLOGUE

'What's this, then?'

The two men were in the roof of the cottage, working on the attic that was to be made into a bedroom. The floor was white with the plaster they had chipped away from the walls. Cobwebs trickled from the rafters. One of the men, prising a chunk of rotten wood from the window frame, had let fall a small bottle wedged behind. It broke as it touched the floor: greenish glass, with a sediment clinging to it.

The other man touched it with his foot. 'That's old glass, that is.'

'This is an old place. Look at the thickness of that wall. And the chimney goes right up through.'

The man who had dropped the bottle pushed the fragments of glass to one side, among plaster chunks, and curls of old wallpaper patterned with green leaves. Whistling, he began to cut new wood for the window frame.

'There's a gap under that frame. Where the old wood come out.'

'I'll plaster it over.'

'Nice view out of there. Straight over to the church.'

'And the lock-up. Remind you to keep your nose clean, eh?' The men laughed.

'This room's not been used in years, I'd say.'

'No. There was an old couple lived here before. Didn't need the space. We had to break the door down, first time I come up here with Mrs Harrison, to see what work had to be done on it. Nailed up, it was. The dust was that thick it was like no one had been up here in a hundred years.'

'Make a nice room when we've done.'

'For the boy, she said. Room of his own, like.'

'We'll get cleared up, I want to get down to the allotment tonight.'

They began to stack tools, sweep the rubbish into a corner. Dust swirled like smoke in the shaft of evening sunlight from the small window: rolls of it drifted over the floor, clinging to the men's feet and overalls.

'Draughty in here.'

'We'll have to see to that window. It wants refitting.'

The men picked up their tools and clattered down the wooden stairs. The door banged behind them, shaking more plaster from the walls, and their footsteps went away down the street. In the room, there was a gathering of air: it bunched and compressed into little winds that nosed the mounds of wallpaper, rustled them, and set the windows faintly rattling. Then it subsided, and the room was quiet: empty.

2(a) What is the connection between the opening paragraph of the first chapter of the story and the Prologue?

ONE

James Harrison and his mother turned out of Ledsham's main street into a lane that ran between terraced cottages. The lane ended abruptly at a gate and became a footpath which disappeared in a landscape of fields and trees, ridged with the dark lines of hedges. Their own cottage stood at the end: the last house in Ledsham. It was called East End Cottage and they had been living there for two weeks.

James walked five paces behind his mother, carrying her shopping basket, which he disliked because it banged against his bare legs and scratched him where the cane was broken. Also it had things like ladies' tights and cabbages sticking out of it, which was embarrassing. Tim, the dog, walked ten paces behind James. James looked back at him and tried to imagine him as one of those large, shaggy, responsible-looking dogs that carry folded-up newspapers and shopping baskets. Tim, squat, square and mongrel, grinned back, independent and unobliging.

They passed under low eaves encrusted with swallows' nests, hanging above front doors that opened straight on to the pavement. Behind each small window were huge plants in pots, dimly green behind the glass, as though seen underwater, shielding murky rooms. In one, a ginger cat gloated at Tim, who scrabbled at the wall in a frenzy of frustration and evil language.

'Make him come,' said Mrs Harrison. 'He'll give us a bad name. Since we seem to have acquired him now, whether we like it or not.'

Tim had arrived at East End Cottage shortly after the Harrisons. He had been found sitting outside the back door, looking pathetic and homeless, had been fed, and within days had installed himself firmly within the house, establishing his rights and ingratiating himself with Mrs Harrison who he was quick to identify as the source of food. He was, clearly, a dog with a long, complicated and mysterious past. Sometimes other people in the village glanced at him curiously, as though they could not quite place him. The postman said he could swear he'd lived at the butcher's at one time and Mr Harrison said grimly that didn't surprise him in the least.

James looped the belt of his jeans through Tim's collar and pulled him away. Tim immediately drooped his stumpy tail and assumed his ill-treated dog pose, for the benefit of an old lady watching from over the street.

'Huh,' said James. 'You don't fool me, you know.' He caught up with his mother.

'Anything for tea?'

'Food,' said Mrs Harrison. 'As usual. I'll have the basket now. Thank you for carrying it.'

'Not at all,' said James politely. He had just embarked on a policy of insurance against various crimes he was certain to commit before long, either with or without intending to. His mother gave him a startled look.

They were almost home now. James could see the window of his attic room, staring over towards the church. The cottage was small, square and comfortable: coming to live in it had been like putting on an old coat. It had a sagging slate roof, a bulge at one end where once there had been a bread-oven, huge beams, creaking stairs, and stone floors with interesting cracks from which emerged, at night, large and stately black beetles. James was making a study of the black beetles: it was going to be called *The Life Cycle of a British Beetle* by Dr James Harrison, FRS, MP, DPhil, OBE. Helen preferred the new houses in the estate the other side of Ledsham, where she already had a network of friends.

'They've got tiled bathrooms, and fitted kitchens. And carpet all the way up the stairs. You ought to see, Mum.'

'I'm sure they're very enviable, dear. But your father and I rather fancied the cottage.'

Mum could be quite sensible about some things, you had to admit that. It makes you wonder, James thought bitterly, what she had to have Helen for. I mean, when you think of all the people she might have had, and she had to have Helen. Other people's sisters were pretty fearful too, but Helen beat the lot. Tiled bathrooms...Ugh!

Helen, of course, had never discovered that you could climb the apple tree that overhung the back of the house and get from thence on to the ledge of the chimney stack. And she'd not noticed the possibilities of the rubbish heap at the far end of the orchard, full of stuff chucked out by the workmen, which he had yet to examine properly. And only he and Tim knew about the nettle-covered well by the fence, where, they strongly suspected, there were rats.

They had seventeen apple trees, instead of the lawn and flower-beds favoured by Helen.

Splendid apple trees, with writhing twisted branches like a troupe of weird dancers frozen amid the long grass. The trees were sagging now, in autumn, with ripe fruit. Mrs Harrison, who was a practical person, had stuck a blackboard up outside the cottage. They could see it now, as they came towards the gate, propped up against the hedge. It said, in white chalk:

Bramleys –   5p. per pound
Worcesters – 6p. per pound
Windfalls –   3p. per pound

And underneath it said:

Sorcerie
Astrologie
Geomancie
Alchemie
Recoverie of Goodes Loste
Physicke

Mrs Harrison put down the basket and read it through carefully. 'Very funny,' she said. 'Very witty. Though the spelling is a little archaic, if I may say so. I suppose I was asking for something like that, putting that board up. And now would you mind wiping it off before tea.' She went up the path and into the cottage. From within came the monotonous sound of Helen playing with a friend.

James studied the blackboard. Not Helen, certainly not Helen. Dad? But the blackboard had not been tampered with when Mr Harrison left in the morning, and he would not be back till later. So who, then? Somebody, thought James, bristling, having a go at me. There's that boy down the road. Simon something. Or one of the other boys at school. How did they know all those words, though? You'd have needed a dictionary for that lot. I'm going to have to sort this out, he thought, later.

3(a) What does 'archaic' mean? (How can you work out the meaning of this word from the rest of this chapter, without using a dictionary?)
(b) Can you find out what 'Sorcerie', 'Astrologie', 'Geomancie' and 'Physicke' might mean?

He followed Tim round the back of the cottage, remembering some unfinished business they had with a hole between the roots of one of the apple trees. They were trying to see if it was possible to mine one's way right under one of the trees and come up the other side. Tim, whatever his other shortcomings, was always game for that kind of thing: indeed, insofar as it is possible for a dog to do so, he even made suggestions himself.

They did some more work on their hole and then, finding themselves thwarted by a large root, decided to come in for tea. Helen and her friend, a pale girl with plaits, no doubt from the world of fitted kitchens and carpeted stairs, were already seated at the table. They watched him come in with a disapproving stare.

'That's my brother,' said Helen. The friend nodded sympathetically.

There were scones and swiss roll. James sat down, feeling cheerful and hungry.

'Mother,' said Helen loudly. 'I do think James might wash his hands before he comes in to tea. Specially when I've got a visitor.' Calling Mum 'mother' was a new idea of hers: she thought it elegant. James glared at her.

'Point taken,' said Mrs Harrison. 'Go and wash them, James.'

He stamped up to the bathroom, and washed the backs of his hands, leaving the palms untouched. Helen needn't think she could win a total victory. His face, freckled, thatched with thick, butter-coloured hair, grinned at him from the mirror: he tried out some of his expressions, the bad-man-in-Western sneer, the Cup-Final captain's grin (holding Cup, or rather, tooth-mug, in upstretched arms), the boxing-champion's snarl (quite good, that one, with towel round neck and hair damped back). Overhead, in his bedroom, he heard a thump. That would be Tim, no doubt. He wasn't supposed to go into the bedrooms, since he made untidy nests on the beds, but there was no known way of stopping him. He was believed to have discovered how to open doors.

His mother's voice came up the stairs. 'James! I said "wash", not have a bath. We're waiting.'

He took the towel off hastily, arranged it on top of the half-open door as a Helen-trap, and hurried downstairs, saying 'Coming, mother.'

Sorry, mother.'

'That'll do,' said Mrs Harrison. 'I'm beginning to feel like a lady in a Victorian novel. Any more of that and I'll get you a frilly shirt and satin knickerbockers.'

Helen and the friend tittered. Something with the bristly texture of a pan-cleaner rubbed against James' leg: it was Tim, dropping hints about the swiss roll. James gave him a puzzled glance. Had he learned to fly, too?

'More cake?' said Mrs Harrison. 'Julia? Helen? No, James, that is the cake, not the slice, if you don't mind. What are you girls planning to do after tea?'

They exchanged looks and began to giggle. 'We'll tell you later,' said Helen, in a heavy whisper. James arranged his face into what he hoped was an expression of deep, searing contempt. That was one of the things about girls—one of the many, many things—this business of going all secret and ridiculous and pretending they were up to something when you knew perfectly well they were too dim to get up to anything at all except some daft business messing about in the kitchen. He sighed deeply, and stared out of the window, with the preoccupied look of someone who has real concerns.

'And you, James? Oh, but you have a job to do, haven't you? That board.'

'We knew it was you,' said Helen. 'We thought it was silly.'

James closed his eyes and assumed an expression of tired resignation.

'Pointless. I s'pose that's why you were late for school.'

James opened one eye and looked balefully at her.

'Not again, James,' said Mrs Harrison.

'And it was all spelt wrong, anyway,' Helen went on.

'All right, then,' said James, goaded beyond endurance. 'Bet *you* don't know what astrology means.'

'I do.'

'What, then?'

'Not telling you,' said Helen.

James said 'Huh'. He fetched the dishcloth from the sink, damped it under the tap, and went out to the gate. Scrubbing the unwanted writing from the board, he thought that whoever had done it had really made rather a good job of it with those curly s's and funny e's. It looked a bit like the writing on old stones, or memorials in churches. All the same, he'd have to find out who it was. You couldn't have people coming along and doing that kind of thing without asking: that was cheek. I'll start with that Simon person, he thought, I bet it was him. He'd noticed him vaguely at school, a short, stumpy boy with immensely thick, round glasses.

He dampened the dishcloth a bit more in a puddle and arranged it on the saddle of Helen's bike. Then he set off for Simon's house, which was at the other end of the lane, towards the High Street.

Simon was conveniently available outside his house, lying along the top of a stone wall. His bespectacled face stared down at James like an amiable gargoyle. 'Hello,' he said, in a friendly, unconcealing voice, not at all like someone who has just been responsible for some kind of trick. Unless, of course, he was a skilled actor.

James found himself at a loss. He stared at Simon for a minute, doubtfully, and then said, with less conviction than he had intended, 'Very funny joke. Ha ha.'

'What?' said Simon.

'Very funny. What you wrote on my mum's blackboard. Very humorous.'

'Hang on,' said Simon. He took off his glasses, which were deeply encrusted with dirt, and rubbed them on his shirt-sleeve, as though a clearer view of the world might help him to understand better. He put them on again and said, 'What blackboard?'

'*You* know.'

'No, I don't.'

'The one outside our house.'

'Let's see,' said Simon, sliding down from the wall.

'I've rubbed it off now. Have you got a pencil?'

Simon felt in his pocket and fished out a chocolate label and slightly chewed biro. James leaned the paper on a brick and wrote, as nearly as he could remember, the words. 'There!'

Simon peered at them thoughtfully, 'It wasn't me,' he said. 'I promise. For a start I don't know what they mean. Except Sorcerie—that's obvious. And Physicke – that's old-fashioned language for medicine. And Recoverie of Goodes Loste just means finding things, I suppose. Anyway,' he went on with disarming honesty, 'I couldn't have spelt them.'

'They're spelt wrong, actually,' said James.

'Oh, are they?'

James studied Simon. There are some people you feel inclined to believe, whatever they say, and others you don't: Simon, he felt, belonged to the first lot.

'Honestly?' he said. 'Swear?'

'Swear.'

'Who do you think it was then? Someone from school?'

'I dunno,' said Simon vaguely. 'Might have been.' He seemed to be losing interest in the problem. 'I've climbed your apple trees,' he said. 'Before you came. The people didn't notice. I accidentally ate an apple too. The best ones are on the tree right at the end.'

'I know,' said James. 'Come on. I'll show you my hole, if you like.'

They walked down the lane together. At the gate James paused and looked suspiciously at the apple-board, but all was as it should be. Tim was sitting outside the gate, staring up at James' bedroom window, making unpleasant growling noises in the back of his throat.

'What's up, Tim?' said James.

'He's saying there's someone he doesn't like in that room,' said Simon.

'It's my room. I bet those stupid girls are in there. Helen's always nosing about. I'll just... No, not now, or we won't have time for the hole. I'll see about her later.'

They spent a happy hour or so on the hole, and discovered a way round the root. Then they did some climbing and worked out a new route up the north face of the largest apple tree. Finally they lay down in the long grass and ate as many apples as they could comfortably manage, throwing the cores to Tim who ate them all, not because he liked them but because he was a dog who had learned never to let an opportunity pass, lest one regret it later.

'I'll have to go,' said Simon finally.

'Bye then. See you.'

'See you.'

There was cauliflower cheese for supper: not one of James' favourites. He tried unsuccessfully to share it with Tim under the table, but Tim, perhaps, had overdone it with the apple cores because he rejected the offerings and circled the kitchen restlessly, as though he had something on his mind. Eventually he went out into the garden, growling.

'Shut the back door, James,' said Mrs Harrison. 'This house is draughty, there's no getting away from it. There's been a cold wind round my feet for the last half-hour.'

'Julia's house is ever so warm,' said Helen. 'It's got central heating.'

'I'd sooner have beetles than central heating,' said James. And mice, he added, but under his breath because that was something he was keeping to himself in case it occurred to anyone that they ought to be trapped.

'Typical,' said Helen. 'Do you know, Mum, he's found someone else just like him. Even grubbier, if possible. They were up the apple tree together.'

'How nice,' said Mrs Harrison. 'Now you've both got a friend.'

James remembered that he still had a score to settle with Helen. He accused her of invading his room. Helen, in exaggerated tones of outrage, said she wouldn't be seen dead in his room. James said he *knew* she'd been there, and it wasn't fair. Both appealed to their mother.

'Stop it, both of you,' said Mrs Harrison. 'I'm a mother, not a referee.'

James, struck with the happy thought of his mother in shorts with a whistle round her neck, began to howl with laughter. Helen glowered at him: she took arguments seriously and liked to pursue them to the bitter end.

'And another thing, Mum, he put a filthy dishcloth on my bike saddle and I sat on it and Julia saw. I mean, it's awfully *embarrassing* in front of my friends.'

'I daresay they've got brothers too,' said Mrs Harrison. 'James, you're to leave your sister alone, do you hear?'

But James had already retreated upstairs.

Sitting on the edge of his bed, undressing, he contemplated his room with satisfaction. It was a jolly good room. The walls and ceilings all sloped wildly in different directions, so that it seemed geometrically impossible that they should all come together in the right way to make up a room at all. The floor was crooked: if you put a marble down it would roll very slowly from one end to the other. You had to stoop a little to see out of the window, but there was a good view, over the rooftops of Ledsham, a clutter of slate and thatch, to the square tower of the church, with swallows dipping round it and the odd little building in the old market place that had once been the village jail and was now the Public Library. There was a table, a chest, and a couple of shelves where James kept his books, his fossil collection, his shells, and various other things, including the clay models he'd made at school last week, two of which, he saw with irritation, had been knocked on to the floor. So she had been up here. Liar.

He rearranged the models and got into bed. He reached under the pillow for his Personal Notebook and began to fill in various details for the day. Under the heading 'Financial Situation', he wrote 'Same as yesterday. I owe Simon 1p. now for winning bet about spitting apple pips farthest. He owes me two sherbet sticks. No pocket money till larder window is paid for.' He turned over the page and put 'Weather good. Wind moderate and coming from west (I think. Unless weathercock on church tower is stuck).' The next page was headed 'Food', and he wrote 'Cottage pie for lunch. Smashing. Three helpings. Cauliflower cheese for dinner. It is the only thing Tim will not eat.' He turned over again, to the page headed 'Future plans'. This was always very full. Now he wrote 'Make complete tunnel from one end of orchard to the other. If successful, send plans to people who are going to build Channel Tunnel. Rig up trap to stop Helen getting into my room. Get hold of a dictionary, and look up "alchemy". Train Tim to carry shopping-baskets.'

Then he put the notebook under the pillow once more, turned the light out, and went immediately to sleep.

During the night he woke feeling cold, and found the eiderdown had been twitched off on to the floor. There was a draught, too, from under the door or somewhere. Crossly, he rearranged the bed, and went to sleep again.

4(a) Discuss the impressions you have formed of (i) Helen (ii) Mrs Harrison
(b) In what ways does James resemble his dog?
5 Imagine you were Helen, Simon, or one of James' parents: describe James as he would appear to the character you imagine yourself to be.
6 Imagine you were James writing his notebook. Under the headings
      Success   *Problems*
list, in note-form, the events of the day described in this chapter, then afterwards compare the lists you have made with other members of your group or class.
7 If Helen kept a private notebook too, what do you think she would write in it looking back on the events of this Chapter?
8 Can you think of a good title for this Chapter?
9 In Chapter 2 you will discover that some words have been left out. Make a list of the words you think are missing, then compare your list with other people's. Sometimes several words could be equally appropriate. Explain why you have chosen the words you have listed. Are any of the words suggested by other people better choices than yours? If so, why?

TWO

'Has anyone seen my pipe?' said Mr Harrison.

'On the dresser,' said Mrs Harrison, without looking up from the sink.

'Under the cornflake packet,' said Helen, through a mouthful of toast.

Mr Harrison walked over to the dresser, stood there, returned to the table, lifted the cornflake packet and put it down again, and then said, 'Don't let me make a nuisance of myself. Distract people, or anything like that. What's your suggestion, James?'

'Hall table,' said James. 'Is there any more bacon, Mum?'

'Thank you,' said his father. 'Is that a hard fact, or merely an informed guess? Don't bother to answer.' He went out of the room and could be heard creaking across the hall.

'Before you disappear altogether I want you to do an errand for me this morning, James,' said Mrs Harrison.

'Yes, Mum. Certainly, Mum.' It was just possible, he'd decided, that a sustained policy of helpfulness might do something to cancel out the larder window.

'I want you to take Helen's prescription along to the chemist for me. I forgot it yesterday.'

Indignation overcame diplomacy. 'Gosh, Mum, why can't she do it? It's not fair. After all, it's her cough, isn't it?'

'She's been invited to the Robinsons' for the day. She won't have time. Did you find it?' Mr Harrison had returned.

'I did not.'

'Oh dear, James and I will have a hunt for it while you're out.'

'Slavery,' said James under his breath. Helen was smirking at him across the table.

'What's that, James?' said Mr Harrison.

'Nothing, Dad. I was just saying to Helen I hoped she'd have a lovely day.'

'Ooh. . .' began Helen.

'Well, I'm off now,' said Mr Harrison. 'Goodbye.'

''Bye, Dad. Well, I s'pose I might as well go and get this weedkiller for Helen. I mean cough mixture.'

(a) 'Here's the prescription. Be careful of it.' Mrs Harrison _____ the piece of paper out of the teapot where spare buttons, loose change and vital documents were kept. James stuffed it into his pocket, and went out into the early-morning bustle of Ledsham. It was a very old place, half way between a village and a small town, and had, somehow, the air of being _____ by the present. New housing estates were _____ ing now on two sides of it, but the centre remained as it must always have been with the houses and streets a size _____ than the houses and streets of a modern town. Lorries, and even the tops of cars, rode _____ with the upstairs windows of the terraced cottages: the streets were too narrow, and the corners too _____ , for modern traffic, creating the most _____ ing traffic-jams. James watched one now, with interest, as the Huntley and Palmer lorry became inextricably _____ up with a tractor and trailer at the main crossroads. There were six pubs, most of them called The Swan, two butchers, no supermarkets, a hairdresser's called Style and Elegance, and a huge, brand-new, plate-glass and concrete comprehensive school, where _____ , most of the names on the register were the same as those in the records of Births, Deaths and Marriages in the church which went back nearly five hundred years. The streets had brief, _____ names that talked about the town's past: Acre End Street, Abbey Way, Pound Lane. Lined with small, honey-coloured houses, they _____ away into the countryside, into green, rivery, elm-_____ Oxfordshire.

(b) The tractor and the Huntley and Palmer lorry sorted themselves out and James moved on. It was Saturday: the day _____ ahead, not set aside for anything in particular, full of _____ . I might get on with the hole, James thought, or I might see if Simon's got any better ideas, or I might go and see those archaeologist people who're digging up something at that farm, or I might. . . . He caught sight of his own face in a cottage window, and _____ to make his chattering-ape grimace at it. Music, _____ down from a radio in a room above, reminded him of his Famous Conductor act. He stood on a brick to get a better view of himself, raised his _____ (or rather, bent straw from gutter) nodded curtly to the orchestra, and _____ out his arms to bring in the three thousand massed violins. He was just pushing the hair out of his eyes after a particularly _____ bit when the astonished face of an elderly man behind the glass reminded him that he was not alone. He got down off the brick _____ .

The chemist's was full of people. He had to wait his turn. Once, he spotted Simon passing the window, sandwiched between his parents, wearing _____ , going-to-visit-relations clothes. Poor old Simon. He waved wildly to attract his attention, and then tried to _____ a message of sympathy and see-you-tomorrow-when-it's-all-over. Simon was _____ past before be could respond.

'When you've quite finished,' said the lady behind the counter _____ . 'I'm waiting.'

'Oh, sorry,' said James. 'My Mum says can she have this please.' He felt in his pocket for the prescription and handed it over.

The assistant turned away, glancing at it. Then she stopped, frowned, and looked more closely.

'Here,' she said. 'Someone's been fooling about with this. I can't take it like this.'

'Let's have a look,' said James.

She handed the prescription back to him. Sure enough, at the top it said, in Doctor Larkins' neat handwriting, 'Mist. Pect. Inf., Tinct. Ipecac. m II, Syrup Squill m V, Syrup Tolu. m V, I teaspoonful t.d.s. to be taken twice daily,' which presumably meant cough mixture. But somebody had drawn a bold blue line through that, in biro, and written underneath, in the same crabbed, old-fashioned looking writing as the words on the apple blackboard, 'Take the leaves of Lungwort, which is a herb of Jupiter, boile them and make of them a syrupe which will much ease a coughe. I counsell thee also to saye certeine charmes over the sicke childe.'

James gasped at it.

'You've got a joker in your house,' said the assistant, looking hard at him. 'Next, please.'

James went out on to the pavement, still staring at the prescription. The matter of the blackboard had been one thing – there were various explanations for that which were quite possible – but this was something else altogether. There were only four people who knew that prescriptions were kept in the old black teapot: his father, his mother, Helen and himself. It was unthinkable that either of his parents would tamper with something as important as a prescription, even for an elaborate joke. And the same went for Helen, who took her health with deadly seriousness. That left...

Me, thought James. And I didn't do it. He began to walk home, very slowly.

At the corner of the lane he stopped. He was in a very awkward situation: there was just no getting away from the fact. If he showed the prescription to his mother she would undoubtedly reach the same conclusion as he had just done. But she didn't know that he hadn't done it.

And the trouble is, he thought, that I'm the sort of boy who might do that sort of thing. And she knows that. Because it's the sort of thing I do sometimes.

Bother.

He worried about what to do all the way back to the cottage. And underneath that worry there was the other matter of who *had* done it. Because he was going to have to get to the bottom of it. It looked suspiciously as though someone was getting at him, and he wasn't going to be got at, not without doing something about it.

He took a deep breath and marched into the kitchen, where he could hear his mother slapping a wooden spoon around in a bowl, and humming. At least Helen wouldn't be about – there was that to be thankful for.

Fifteen minutes later he was sitting on the end of his bed, feeling injured and resentful. She hadn't believed him. As she'd pointed out, with some justification, he had to admit, who else could it have been? And the more vehement and truthful he'd tried to be, the more red-faced and untruthful-sounding he'd become, which was most unfair. In fact the whole thing was bitterly unfair: one didn't mind being told off and punished for things one had done – at least not much – but when it came to something that one hadn't done... Glowering, he determined to find out who this rotten person was if it was the last thing he did. He ground the toe of his plimsoll into the rug by his bed: the whole promising day had collapsed in ruins around him. He was to spend it helping her clear out the old shed at the back of the cottage, as a penance. When he'd tidied his room.

Tim was pacing round and round the floor with the hairs along his spine lifted in a dark ridge, exactly as he behaved when in the neighbourhood of the well in the orchard. All of a sudden he sat down on his haunches, facing the table where James did his homework, and barked.

'Shut up,' said James. 'There aren't any rats up here.'

Tim batted his short tail to and fro and barked again. Then he bared his teeth and growled.

'Oh, cut it out,' said James irritably. He began to make the bed, rolling his pyjamas into a ball and stuffing them under the pillow, and smoothing the counterpane over the disaster area underneath. Only an experienced eye would spot the deception, and with any luck his mother wouldn't come up before tonight. He went round the room picking up things that were on the floor and arranging them in piles elsewhere, which is always the most effective way of making a room appear tidy. Even as he did so a pen rolled off the table behind him, and some papers fluttered in the breeze from the open window. How could he be expected to keep his room tidy when things moved about by themselves, huh?

He picked the pen up – his good red biro it was, and it looked as if someone had been mucking about with it – and put it back on the table. All of a sudden something caught his eye. Some red writing on a sheet of paper laid on top of his project book. Not his writing. He picked it up: it looked horribly familiar. Not *again...* It said:

Tell thy father that if he would knowe who hath stollen his pipe he should take a sieve & hange itt from a payre of sheeres & when he name the person he suspecteth the sheeres will turne. Or if he preferre he may use the crystalle. I have been about the towne & I am muche displeased for there are manie who do usurpe my worke & professe to find thieves & give physicke & thou hast in this verie dwellynge a machine which tells if there will be muche sunshine or no. We will be verie busie, thou & I.

The writing was spidery, as though the pen had slid about. At the bottom of the page there was a further line, which said petulantly 'I lyke not this quill'.

James sat down on the bed, because his legs suddenly felt a bit odd. He read it through three times, while Tim went to sleep in the patch of yellow sunlight from the window. Then he did some hard thinking, and came up with some conclusions. Namely, that the writing had not been there when he got up that morning, that therefore it had been done since then, and it could not have been done by either his father or by Helen, since both had come downstairs before he had and had left the house without going up again.

So either his mother was playing an elaborate joke on him – so elaborate, indeed, that one would have to think she had gone absolutely barmy – or someone else had been in the house. Which was rather a creepy idea.

And there were other things, too. Tim, barking at the empty air. Thumps, from a room with nobody in it.

He folded the paper up carefully and put it in the wallet where he kept various important things, like old programmes and entrance tickets and his swimming certificates. Then he went downstairs, feeling thoughtful.

---

10 Imagining yourself to be James, describe what he may have been thinking as he went downstairs. What has annoyed him? What were the 'other things'?

11 Make another entry in James' notebook, listing, in note-form, what has occurred so far in this chapter.

12(a) Rewrite the 'archaic' passage ('Tell thy father... thou and I') in modern English.

(b) What does 'petulantly' mean? (It comes three lines after the 'archaic' passage).

13 Now read the rest of this chapter. Think of a title for it. When you come to another passage with words missing do the same as in 9 above.

Mrs Harrison and James spent the rest of the morning dragging junk out of the shed. It was to be made into a workshop and storeroom. It was not so much a shed, really, as a part of the house, since it was built of the same stone and adjoined it, though the old slate roof had fallen in and been replaced with corrugated iron. Mrs Harrison said she supposed it must once have been a cowshed. The job was less tedious than James had expected, since there were all kinds of interesting things in the shed, like immensely old and complex mousetraps, ancient agricultural implements of tortuous design whose purpose could not even be guessed at, a calendar dating from the first World War, and (joy of joys!) a tin helmet and a gas-mask. James cheered up considerably as the morning progressed. He also probed his mother, cautiously, talking loudly about sieves, shears, and crystals, and asking her how you spelt 'physicke'. To none of this did she respond in any way, except to say would he kindly stop chuntering on about nothing and get on with what he was supposed to be doing.

Finally he said, as casually as he could manage, 'By the way, Mum, did anyone come in while I was at the chemist? Just kind of blow in and wander up the stairs?'

'No,' she said. 'Nobody blew or wandered. Would you like to put all this stuff in a wheelbarrow and take it down to the rubbish heap? No, on second thoughts, dig a hole and bury it.'

Digging the hole took up most of the afternoon. As a professional hole-digger, James took the matter seriously. He made it good and deep, and as he dug it soon became clear that he was digging up someone else's much more ancient rubbish heap, since he kept uncovering bits of broken china and pottery and innumerable small bones, as well as the stems and bowls of clay pipes. One of the advantages of living in a house which had been lived in for a pretty long time was that other people's very interesting rubbish was never far away. After an hour or so he had unearthed a whole sequence of domestic breakages, from eighteenth-century wine-bottles through flowery Victorian cups to twentieth-century Woolworth's blue and white china. The bones, too, would need to be classified: most of them were clearly the remains of long-past Sunday dinners, or the buried treasure of Tim's ancestors, but some at least, he thought hopefully, might turn out to be human. At last he decided the hole would do, and dragged the wheelbarrow to the edge in order to tip the contents into it. Just as he was about to do so he caught sight of a piece of wire protruding from the side of the hole: he stooped down and gave it a tug. It came out with a shower of loose soil and revealed itself to be one arm of a very ancient pair of spectacles. He examined this trophy with much pleasure: the lenses had gone, but the frame was intact – thin, rusty wire with very small eye-pieces, not unlike the National Health ones that Simon wore. He put them in his pocket.

A

By the evening, after a day of reasonably amicable relations with his mother, James felt that the matter of the prescription had been dropped. At least, it was not mentioned again. But as far as he himself was concerned it was not over at all, he had yet to find out who was responsible. He was not going to go on taking the blame for things he hadn't done. Huh...

At supper Mr Harrison said, 'Oh, by the way, I hope you didn't waste a lot of time looking for my pipe. It was in my jacket pocket after all.'

James and his mother looked at each other. 'I must confess we forgot all about it,' said Mrs Harrison.

'Nobody stole it?' said James.

'I never suggested anybody had.'

'What's *he* been doing all day?' said Helen, eyeing James with _____.

'Oh, nothing much,' said James _____. 'Mum took me to a circus this afternoon, and we had home-made ice-cream for lunch. Three helpings each. And this morning we went swimming. It was rather a dull day really. You didn't miss much.'

Helen's eyes grew large and shiny, the signal of approaching tears. She put down her knife and fork and began, _____, 'Oh, it's not fair... Just when I wasn't here....'

'Helen,' said Mrs Harrison, with a sigh, 'we all know that living with James can be very trying. But it does help to develop a resistance to some of his more _____ lines of deception.'

Helen picked up her knife and fork again, with a _____ look at James, who grinned back.

'He's been here all day,' said Mrs Harrison. 'As a matter of fact he was being punished...'

'Crumbs!' said James, leaping to his feet and rushing to the window. 'What's that!'

It worked. Tim flew from under the table and rushed at the door, barking wildly and pulling the cloth half off the table. A glass of water fell over, everybody tried to mop it up and in the general _____ the rest of Mrs Harrison's remark was lost.

'Sorry,' said James, 'thought I saw someone in the garden. Mistake.'

His father gave him the hard stare of a man who had not been taken in, and went through to the sitting-room. James followed, hurriedly turning on the television to _____ any further remarks.

B

Television has many virtues, not the least of them being, James thought, that it provides a continuous _____ to paper over a _____ unreliable situation. The Harrisons settled down for the evening: once, Helen said, 'Where's my new cough mixture?' but her mother's reply was _____ in a burst of gunfire from the Mexican border.

'Ssh,' said James. 'This is good.'

He and Helen lay on their stomachs, side by side, with Tim between them. Tim sat with his head between his paws, facing the television set, eyes half-closed, occasionally twitching. He clearly thought the television screen to be a window beyond which there was a real and _____ world from which he was excluded, peopled with fleeing horses, other dogs, and a host of wild animals. Occasionally, when things got too much for him, he would _____ himself against the glass in an _____ attempt to chase these _____ creatures. He was believed by James and Mr Harrison to _____ a good Western.

'Bed,' said Mrs Harrison, at last.

'In a minute,' said James and Helen in _____.

'As soon as the news is over, then.'

The news ended. The weather forecast began. 'Tomorrow will be cloudy and dull in most parts, with light to moderate winds. Temperatures will be around....'

There was a loud crash from the sideboard. Everybody looked round. The blue vase was lying on the floor in pieces.

'I didn't touch it,' James said quickly. 'I was over here.'

'Nor me,' said Helen. Both children looked at their mother with expressions of deep _____.

'How very peculiar,' said Mrs Harrison, picking up the pieces. 'Luckily it's one I've never cared for. A wedding present.'

'How on earth did it fall off by itself?' said Helen.

'Small local earthquake,' said their father with a yawn. 'Very frequent in this part of Oxfordshire. Up, both of you.' He picked up the newspaper.

James and Helen climbed the stairs slowly, pausing on every step to argue about who was to use the bathroom first. At the top, Helen gave in unexpectedly.

'You have it. Anyway, you need it most,' she added as an after-thought. Then, 'I say, it was funny about that vase, wasn't it?'

'Mmm,' said James, abstractedly.

'Didn't you honestly do it? Not with a string or something?'

'I jolly well did not.'

'All right, all right. I just wondered.'

James, feeling in his pocket for the various objects he had brought in from his hole, felt the rustle of a piece of paper and remembered. For a moment there flitted around in his head the notion of telling Helen about it, even showing her, telling her about the prescription.... There were times when she could be almost human, and he needed help. Then commonsense prevailed: this wasn't the kind of thing you let a mere girl in on, least of all Helen. He creaked up the stairs to his room.

He was a long time getting to bed. First of all he had to clear a shelf for his new treasures: the spectacle frame, the best of the clay pipes (one, indeed, intact except for an inch or so of stem), the pottery sequence, and various buttons and pieces of bone. He was planning a small exhibition, to be called 'Three Hundred Years of Domestic Life in an Oxfordshire Cottage'. Then, when he'd done that there was the notebook to be filled in (under 'Future Plans' he wrote in block capitals FIND OUT WHO IS PLAYING TRICKS ON ME AND JOLLY WELL SORT HIM OUT), and then at last he was able to get into bed.

He was lying there, telling himself a long and elaborate story about a shipwreck in which he was all the characters by turn, when it suddenly appeared to him that all was not right with the mirror above the table. There was writing on it. He shot out of bed and bounced across the room. Oh *no*....

There was a further message, scrawled greasily on the mirror in (oh, horror!) his mother's lipstick. James read it with a mixture of indignation and mounting amazement.

Wee must take paines to informe thy neighboures that I doe once more practise my arte and cunninge in this howse. There is much businesse for us in the towne: I fancie manie doe practise witcherie. Tell thy familie they shall knowe what the weather will be from me & not from that eville machine or I will breake more pots. I perceive thou hast dygged up my spectacles & my pipe. It was my first apprentice loste them in the yarde: he was a scoundrell & a lazie fellow & I had often cause to beate him. Take care that thou serve me better.

Surprisingly, James slept well. When he woke in the morning the church bells were ringing and the streets were Sunday-ish and quiet, with people cleaning cars instead of driving them and old ladies walking past in gloves and hats. For a moment he couldn't think what it was that nagged somewhere in his head, like a forgotten message or an undiscovered crime, and then he caught sight of the writing on the mirror, and everything came back with a rush. The writing had lost its initial impact now and merely looked scruffy. He rubbed it off with a handkerchief and got back into bed again to think about things.

Sorcerie, astrologie, physicke. . . .

Thou hast dygged up my spectacles. . . .

He's got a very weird way of saying things, this person. Old-fashioned. Unless it's somebody putting it on, but it doesn't sound like that.

Nobody but me knows about the spectacles, because as it happens I didn't show them to anyone. Therefore they must have been his spectacles, or he couldn't have known about them.

If someone has spectacles, they are a real person. But those are very old specs.

It was my first apprentice lost them in the yard. . . .

The person who's writing these messages, thought James carefully, is someone who once lived in this house. He's getting in, somehow, without anyone noticing, and doing it. To have a go at me. For some reason. Because he's barmy or something.

He's getting in and wandering around, and doing all this, and there are four of us living here and none of us have noticed him.

'No,' he said out loud, 'No.' He got out of bed and dressed, slowly.

Tim goes mad every time anyone comes near the house. Postmen, and milkmen. He'd know. But he has been barking. At nothing.

He said firmly, aloud, 'It's impossible. There aren't such things!' and went downstairs.

14(a) What can James do now? Could his interest in archaeology be of help to him?
(b) Imagine James trying to tell his father, mother, sister and friend about what has happened: what would each of them say in reply?
15 Discuss what you have found amusing in these chapters.
16(a) Can you explain what has happened? What does James mean when he says 'It's impossible. There aren't such things'?
(b) Read the Prologue again. Is there any clue there?

Appendix

Suggestions for further reading

Joan Aiken *Collections of Short Stories*
Antonia Barber *The Amazing Mr Blunden*
Nina Bawden *A Handful Of Thieves: The Peppermint Pig*
Betsy Byars *The Eighteenth Emergency*
Peter Carter *Under Goliath*
John Christopher *The Lotus Caves: The Prince In Waiting*
Arthur C Clarke *Of Time and Stars*
Susan Cooper *Dawn of Fear:* The *Dark Is Rising* sequence
Peter Dickinson The *Changes* trilogy
Eilis Dillon *The Island Of Horses*
Gertie Evenhuis *What About Me?*
Penelope Farmer *Charlotte Sometimes*
Nicholas Fisk *Grinny: Trillion*
Leon Garfield *The Stange Affair Of Adelaide Harris*
Jean George *My Side Of The Mountain*
Nigel Hinton *Collision Course*
Anne Holm *I Am David*
Harry Harrison *The Man From P.I.G.*
Clive King *The Night The Water Came*
Diana Wynne Jones *Charmed Life*
Ursula LeGuin The *Earthsea* trilogy
Julius Lester *Long Journey Home*
Penelope Lively *The Ghost of Thomas Kempe*
Jan Mark *Thunder and Lightnings: Under The Autumn Garden*
William Mayne *Earthfasts*
Robert O'Brien *Mrs Frisby and the Rats of NIMH*
Scott O'Dell *Island of the Blue Dolphin*
K M Peyton *Flambards*
Charles G D Roberts *Red Fox*
Andrew Salkey *Eearthquake*
Ivan Southall *Ash Road: Let The Balloon Go*
Rosemary Sutcliff *Blood Feud: Dragonslayer: The Eagle of the Ninth*
Geraldine Symons *Mademoiselle: The Workhouse Child*
Theodore Taylor *The Cay*
Henry Treece *Legions of the Eagle: Viking's Dawn: Horned Helmet*
Jill Paton Walsh *The Dolphin Crossing*
Barba Willard *The Mantlemass Series*